HRH Princess Alice, Duchess of Gloucester

SGS has lost a charming and remarkably long-lived President. Former members of the Executive Committee and District Organisers will remember HRH fondly and gratefully, for the interest and support she gave to the Scheme in past times.

I had the honour of lunching with Princess Alice at Barnwell, the home and garden she loved. After lunch she lent me her second pair of muddy gum boots and we set off on a glorious tour of her own beautiful garden. HRH was a proper 'hands on' gardener and could not pass a weed!

She wanted to show me the jardinières that SGS had given her to mark its Diamond Jubilee in 1991 and show me how pretty they looked by the pool.

Princess Alice liked to hear news and chat about the Scheme and hear how everything was going, when she was well in to her nineties.

I believe that we came quite high on her huge list of charities because Scotland remained her home, in her heart, and gardening was such a great interest.

We have been extremely fortunate to have had HRH as our President for 67 years.

Mrs S Luczyc - Wyhowska
Vice President

GARDENS OF SCOTLAND 2005

Contents

FRONT COVER PHOTOGRAPH
Hellebores (Ashwood hybrids)
Photographer - Ray Cox

Printed by Inglis Allen, 40 Townsend Place, Kirkcaldy, Fife.

Chairman's Message

We were greatly saddened by the deaths last year of our President HRH Princess Alice, Duchess of Gloucester who had been associated with Scotland's Gardens Scheme, through the QNIS, since we were formed in 1931 and our Vice-President and Past Chairman Barbara Findlay whose enthusiasm for SGS was an inspiration to us all. You will find appreciations of them elsewhere in this book.

By buying our yellow book and enjoying some of the most wonderful gardens which our garden owners are kind enough to invite us to visit you will be helping us, I hope, to achieve another record year in 2005. We know that our principle beneficiaries and the many other charities which our garden owners support use your money wisely and thank you all for your generosity.

Charlotte Hunt

SCOTLAND'S GARDENS SCHEME

A registered Scottish charity founded in 1931 to support the Queen's Nursing Institute Scotland - see page 6.

Over 350 gardens of all sizes open to the public on one or more days each year.

Garden owners donate entry fees and revenue from teas and plant sales to support our beneficiaries.

The Gardens Fund of the National Trust for Scotland became our second principal beneficiary in 1952 - see page 7.

We also support Perennial (GRBS) and the Royal Gardeners' Orphan Fund - see page 8.

In 2004 149 registered charities of the owners' choice received up to 40% of the day's takings;

145 volunteers work in 27 Districts throughout Scotland to help the Scheme.

One six day tour to gardens is run every year.

In 2004 £217,344 was distributed to charities.

THE QUEEN'S NURSING INSTITUTE SCOTLAND
Patron: Her Majesty The Queen

31 Castle Terrace Edinburgh EH1 2EL
Tel 0131 229 2333   Fax 0131 228 9066

Registered Charity SC005751

Founded by Royal Charter in 1889, the Queen s Nursing Institute trained and supervised District Nurses throughout Scotland, until 1970 and assisted in the setting up of District Nursing Associations.   Since then it has worked to educate, promote and support Community Nurses in primary care.

The Queen s Nursing Institute is a registered charity concerned with the welfare of over 700 Queen s Nurses on the mailing list.

The following projects are currently being funded – made possible by the generous donation from Scotland's Gardens Scheme.   Each of these projects focuses on current unmet needs within the community.

Gerontology Project

The QNIS supported a competition to celebrate the achievements, as well as highlight and share good practice, of the Gerontology Demonstration Project. Funding has been also awarded this year for developing Best Practice Statements for maximising communication with older people with a hearing disability.

GOPIP

The GOPIP project goes from strength to strength, and this Refugee Nurses Returning to Work Project has successfully provided adaptation courses and supervised practical experience for overseas nurses seeking refugee status in Scotland. An extra year s funding was granted to coincide with NHS Education funding.

Multi-agency Leadership Development Programme

An award was made towards the provision of a Multi-agency leadership development programme, called Challenge to Change , for nurses working on Islay and Mull.

CD ROM Dementia Learning Resource

An award was given to the Dementia Services Development Centre towards the development of a CD ROM Dementia Learning Resource, for practice nurses, district nurses and health visitors.

Welfare of Retired Queen's Nurses

Continuing support and care for retired Queen s Nurses who have given much of their time and effort to the community.   Pensions, visiting schemes, special grants, group holidays, newsletters and annual gatherings are offered to retired Queen s Nurses.

Chairman: Sir David Carter MD, FRCS(Ed), FRSE
Nurse Director: Mrs Julia Quickfall, MSc, B.Nurs., SRN., DN., Hv Cert, MIHM

The National Trust
for Scotland

A Message to Garden Owners from The National Trust for Scotland

November 2004

Perhaps we should regard the vagaries of the weather this summer, in contrast to the spectacular sunshine of last year, as ultimately being of benefit to our gardens and plant collections, permitting them the opportunity to redress the imbalance of drought conditions. Landslides and floods are possibly not exactly one's chosen preference.

In spite of these climatic extremes your garden owners have once again triumphed in what, through their efforts long before they open their gardens, they have raised and once again The National Trust for Scotland is hugely grateful for the amount of continuous support which we receive through Scotland's Gardens Scheme. This donation benefits many areas of the Trust's gardens community and steadily underpins the variety of opportunities we can undertake within many of our gardens. More than this, it also goes towards unexpected emergency work such as that of footpath repair work such as at Crarae Garden where flooding had seriously eroded some of the paths. At Brodick Castle there has been urgent tree-work which has also benefitted from your wonderful support.

Next year, 2005, we are planning celebrations for 60 years of Gardens in The National Trust for Scotland and this will be a golden opportunity for special events at our properties and for events which we might share in together. We look forward to taking this as an opportunity to involve Scotland's Gardens Scheme wherever we possibly can, for our mutual benefit, and we look forward to welcoming you to many of our gardens especially under Scotland's Garden Scheme Open Days.

We wish you another equally successful season in 2005, maybe with a return to a summer of unending sunshine with overnight rain at perfect intervals.

Robin Pellew

Dr Robin Pellew
Chief Executive

THE THE
ROYAL GARDENERS'
ORPHAN FUND

THE ROYAL GARDENERS' ORPHAN FUND

Registered Charity No: 248746

The RGOF has been helping orphaned children of professional horticulturists since 1887. We can also offer support to needy children whose parents are employed in horticulture, whether the need be through illness, disability, or in times of particular financial hardship. This assistance takes the form of regular quarterly allowances to orphaned children; grants towards such items as winter clothing, school uniforms, beds and bedding for those in need; and specialised equipment for disabled children.

Over the past year we have helped three orphaned children in Scotland — two boys of fourteen and thirteen and their older sister who has now gone on to further education. We have helped a further eight needy children with school uniform and winter clothing. We find that whilst many of the families we help can just manage on a day to day basis, the added cost of school and winter clothing is beyond their reach and it is here that our help is most needed.

The support we receive from Scotland s Gardens Scheme is much appreciated and enables our work in Scotland to continue.

If you would like further information regarding our work please contact our Secretary, Mrs Kate Wallis, at 14 Scholars Mews, Welwyn Garden City, Herts, AL8 7JQ, or visit our website at www.rgof.org.uk.

GENERAL INFORMATION

Maps. The maps show the *approximate* locations of gardens – directions can be found in the garden descriptions or full maps on the web site at *www.gardensofscotland.org*

Houses are not open unless specifically stated; where the house or part of the house is shown, an additional charge is usually made.

Lavatories. Private gardens do not normally have outside lavatories. For security reasons, owners have been advised not to admit visitors into their houses.

Dogs. Unless otherwise stated, dogs are usually admitted, but only if kept on a lead. They are not admitted to houses.

Teas. When teas are available this is indicated in the text. An extra charge is usually made for refreshments.

Professional Photographers. No photographs taken in a garden may be used for sale or reproduction without the prior permission of the garden owner.

 ♿ Denotes gardens suitable for wheelchairs.

 ✿ Shows gardens opening for the first time or re-opening after many years.

The National Trust for Scotland. Members please note that where a National Trust property has allocated an opening day to Scotland's Gardens Scheme which is one of its own normal opening days, members can gain entry on production of their Trust membership card, although donations to Scotland's Gardens Scheme will be most welcome.

Children. All children must be accompanied by an adult.

SCOTLAND'S GARDENS SCHEME

Charity No. SC011337

We welcome gardens large and small and also groups of gardens.
If you would like information on how to open your garden for
charity please contact us at the address below.

SCOTLAND'S GARDENS SCHEME,
22 RUTLAND SQUARE, EDINBURGH EH1 2BB
Telephone: 0131 229 1870   Fax: 0131 229 0443
E-mail: *office@sgsgardens.fsnet.co.uk*

NAME & ADDRESS: (Block capitals please)

....

....

....

Postcode............................... Tel:...

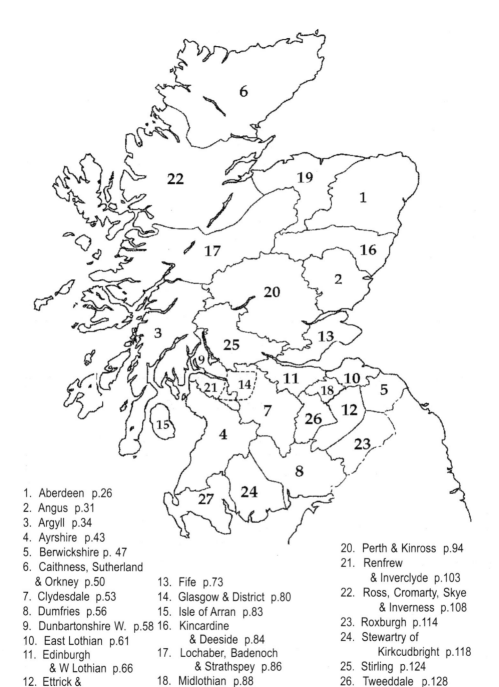

Gardens Open on a Regular Basis or By Appointment
Full details are given in the District List of Gardens

ABERDEEN

Blairwood, Aberdeen .... June – October by appointment
23 Don Street, Old Aberdeen .... June – August by appointment
Grandhome, Aberdeen .... By appointment
Greenridge, Cults .... July & August by appointment
Hatton Castle, Turriff .... By appointment
Howemill, Craigievar .... By appointment
Ploughman's Hall, Old Rayne .... By appointment
Waterside Farmhouse, Oyne .... By appointment

ANGUS

House of Pitmuies, Guthrie, by Forfar .... 1 April - 31 October
.... 10am - 5pm

ARGYLL

Achnacloich, Connel .... Daily 25 March - 31 Oct 10am - 6pm
An Cala, Ellenabeich .... Daily 1 April - 31 October 10am - 6pm
Ardchattan Priory, North Connel. .... Daily 1 April - 31 October 9am - 6pm
Ardkinglas Woodland Garden .... Daily all year round
.... daylight hours
Ardmaddy Castle, by Oban .... Daily all year 9am - sunset
Ardno, Cairndow .... By appointment
Ascog Hall, Isle of Bute .... Daily (except Mons & Tues)
.... Easter - End October 10am - 5pm
Barguillean's "Angus Garden" .... Daily all year 9am - 6pm
Cnoc-na-Garrie, Ballymeanoch .... Daily 25 Mar - 31 Oct
.... (Closed Mon & Tues) 10am - 6pm
Coille Dharaich, Kilmelford .... By appt most days 15 April - 15 Sept
Druimavuic House, Appin .... Daily April, May & June 10am - 6pm
Druimneil House, Port Appin .... Daily 1 April - 31 October 9am - 6pm
Eckford, By Dunoon .... Daily 9 April - 6 June 10am - 5pm
Glecknabae, Isle of Bute .... By appointment Spring - Autumn
Jura House, Ardfin, Isle of Jura. .... Open all year 9am - 5pm
Kildalloig, Campbeltown .... By appointment

Kinlochlaich House Gardens, Appin. .... *Open all year   9.30 -5.30 or dusk*
.... *Except Suns Oct - Mar   Suns Apr - Sept*
.... *10.30am - 5.30pm*
Torosay Castle Gardens, Isle of Mull .... *Gardens open all year*
26 Kilmartin, Lochgilphead............................ *01 June - 30 Sept Mon & Thurs & by appt.*
.... *10.30am - Dusk*

BERWICKSHIRE
Bughtrig, Leitholm .... *15 June – 15 September 11am – 5pm, or by appt*
Manderston, Duns .... *Suns & Thurs 8 May – 29 September 2 - 5pm*
Netherbyres, Eyemouth .... *Parties of 10 or more by appt at any time*

CAITHNESS, SUTHERLAND & ORKNEY
Kerrachar, Kylesku .... *Mid May - mid Sept Tues, Thurs & Suns*
.... *& By Appt.*
Langwell, Berriedale .... *By appointment*

CLYDESDALE
Baitlaws, Lamington .... *By appointment June, July, August*
Biggar Park, Biggar .... *Groups May - July by appointment*
Culter Allers, Coulter .... *By appointment*
Drakelaw Pottery, Crawfordjohn .... *By appointment*

DUNBARTONSHIRE WEST
Auchendarroch, Tarbet.................................... *By appointment*
Glenarn, Rhu .... *Daily 21 Mar - 21 Sept Sunrise - sunset*

EAST LOTHIAN
Inwood, Carberry .... *Tues, Thurs & Sats 1 Apr - 30 Sept 2 - 5pm*
.... *Groups by appt. Tel: (0131) 665 4550*
Shepherd House, Inveresk .... *Tues & Thurs 2 - 4pm Apr, May & June*
.... *& By appointment Tel: 0131 665 2570*
Stobshiel House, Humbie .... *By appointment Tel: 01875 833646*
.... *email: wardhersey@aol.com*

EDINBURGH
61 Fountainhall Road, Edinburgh .... *By appointment*
Newliston, Kirkliston...................................... *Wed - Suns inc. 1 May - 4 June*
.... *2 - 6pm*

FIFE

Cambo House, Kingsbarns .... *Open all year 10am - dusk*
Strathtyrum, St Andrews .... *Weekdays 1st week of May, June, July,*
.... *August & September 2 - 4pm*

GLASGOW

Invermay, Cambuslang .... *April - September by appointment*

LOCHABER, BADENOCH & STRATHSPEY

Ardtornish, Lochaline, Morvern .... *Open 1 April - 31 October 10am - 6pm*

MIDLOTHIAN

Newhall, Carlops .... *By appointment 01968 660206*

MORAY & NAIRN

Knocknagore, Knockando .... *By appointment*

PERTH & KINROSS

Ardvorlich, Lochearnhead .... *1 May to 5 June All day*
Bolfracks, Aberfeldy .... *1 April - 31 October 10am - 6pm*
Bradystone House, Murthly .... *May, June & July by appointment*
Braco Castle, Braco .... *1 February - 31 October by appointment*
Cluniemore, Pitlochry .... *1 May - 1 Oct and by appointment*
Cluny House, Aberfeldy .... *1 March - 31 October 10am - 6pm*
Glendoick, by Perth .... *11 April - 10 June Mon - Fri 10 am - 4pm*
Monkmyre, Coupar Angus .... *1 June - 30 September by appointment*
Rossie House, Forgandenny .... *1 March - 31 October by appointment*
Rossie Priory, Inchture .... *1 March - 31 September by appointment*
Scone Palace, Perth .... *25 March - 31 October 9.30 - 5pm*
Wester Dalqueich, Carnbo .... *1 May - 31 August by appointment*

ROSS, CROMARTY, SKYE & INVERNESS

Abriachan, Loch Ness Side .... *February - November 9am - dusk*
An Acarsaid, Ord, Isle of Skye .... *April - October 10am - 5.30pm*
Attadale, Strathcarron .... *1 Apr - end Oct Closed Suns 10am - 5.30pm*
Balmeanach House, Struan .... *Weds & Sats end Apr - mid Oct 11am - 4.30pm*
Coiltie Garden, Divach, Drumnadrochit .... *14 May - 23 July Noon - 7pm*
Dunvegan Castle, Isle of Skye .... *21 March - 31 October 10am - 5.30pm*

Leckmelm Shrubbery & Arboretum .... *1 April - 31 October 10am - 6pm*
The Hydroponicum, Achiltibuie .... *March - 30 Sep & Mon - Fri in Oct*

ROXBURGH

Floors Castle, Kelso .... *Open daily from 3 Apr to 31 Oct 10am - 4.30pm*

STEWARTRY OF KIRKCUDBRIGHT

Barnhourie Mill, Colvend .... *May - Oct by appointment*
Carleton Croft, Borgue .... *July to August by appointment*
Danevale Park, Crossmichael .... *By appointment*
Southwick House, Dumfries .... *27 June - 1 July*

STIRLING

14 Glebe Crescent, Tillicoultry .... *By appointment*
Ballindalloch, Balfron .... *By appt May and June*
Callander Lodge, Callander .... *By appointment*
Camallt, Fintry .... *By appointment*
Daldrishaig House, Aberfoyle .... *By appointment*
Gargunnock House, Gargunnock .... *Weds mid April - mid June & in Sept & Oct*
.... *and By appointment*
Kilbryde Castle, Dunblane .... *By appointment*

TWEEDDALE

Kailzie Gardens, Peebles .... *Open all year round*

WIGTOWN

Ardwell House Gardens, Ardwell .... *Daily 1 April - 30 September 10am - 5pm*
Logan House Gardens, Port Logan .... *Daily 1 February - 1 April 10am - 4pm*
.... *2 April - 31 August 9am - 6pm*

MONTHLY LIST

FULL DETAILS ARE GIVEN IN THE DISTRICT LIST OF GARDENS

To be announced

Edinburgh & W. Lothian .... Dalmeny Park, South Queensferry
Stewartry of Kircudbright .... Danevale Park, Crossmichael

Sunday 13 February

Renfrew & Inverclyde .... Ardgowan, Inverkip

Wednesday 23 February

Fife .... Cambo Snowdrops, Kingsbarns

Sunday 27 February

Renfrew & Inverclyde .... Auchengrange & Lochside, Lochwinnoch

Sunday 6 March

East Lothian .... Smeaton Hepburn, East Linton

Sunday 3 April

East Lothian .... Winton House, Pencaitland
Edinburgh & W. Lothian .... 61 Fountainhall Road, Edinburgh

Sunday 10 April

Berwickshire .... Netherbyres, Eyemouth
Dumfries .... Dalswinton House, Auldgirth
Fife .... Wemyss Castle, Wemyss
Perth & Kinross .... Megginch Castle, Errol
Stewartry of Kircudbright .... Senwick House, Brighouse Bay

Wednesday 14 April

Ross, Cromarty, Skye & Inverness .... Dundonnell House, Dundonnell, by Garve

Saturday 16 April

Ross, Cromarty, Skye & Inverness .... Inverewe, Poolewe

Sunday 17 April

East Lothian .... Lennoxlove, Haddinton
Edinburgh & W. Lothian .... Foxhall, Kirkliston
Ettrick & Lauderdale .... Bemersyde, Melrose
Fife .... Cambo Plant Fair, Kingsbarns

Renfrew & Inverclyde .... Finlaystone, Langbank
Tweeddale .... Barns, Kirkton Manor

Sunday 24 April
Argyll .... Benmore Botanic Garden, Dunoon
Dunbartonshire West .... Kilarden, Rosneath
Midlothian .... Oxenfoord Castle, Pathhead
Moray & Nairn .... Knocknagore, Knockando
Perth & Kinross .... Cleish, Kinross (Cleish Castle & Boreland)
Stirling .... The Pass House, Kilmahog
Stirling .... Touch, Stirling

Saturday 30 April
Argyll .... Strachur House Woodland Garden

Sunday 1 May
Argyll .... Strachur House Woodland Garden
Ayrshire .... Glendoune, Girvan
Clydesdale .... Nemphlar Garden Trail, Nemphlar
Dunbartonshire West .... Glenarn, Rhu
Perth & Kinross .... Glendoick, by Perth
Stewartry of Kircudbright .... Walton Park, Castle Douglas
Stirling .... Brioch, Kippen
Wigtown .... Logan House Gardens, Port Logan

Saturday 7 May
Argyll .... Crinan Hotel Garden, Crinan
Argyll .... Arduoine, Kilmelford

Sunday 8 May
Argyll .... Arduoine, Kilmelford
Dumfries .... Portrack House, Holywood
East Lothian .... Aberlady Village
Edinburgh & W. Lothian .... Moray Place & Bank Gardens, Edinburgh
Edinburgh & W. Lothian .... South Queensferry Gardens
Fife .... Parleyhill & Culross Manse
Perth & Kinross .... Branklyn, Perth
Ross, Cromarty, Skye & Inverness Allangrange, Munlochy
Stewartry of Kircudbright .... Carstramont, Gatehouse of Fleet
Stirling .... Southwood Gardeners' Market, Stirling

Saturday 14 May
Argyll .... Colintraive Gardens

Sunday 15 May

Angus	Brechin Castle, Brechin
Ayrshire	Avonmill Cottage, Drumclog
Argyll	Colintraive Gardens
Argyll	Achara House, Duror of Appin
Dumfries	Dalswinton House, Auldgirth
Dunbartonshire West	Geilston Garden, Cardross
East Lothian	Shepherd House, Inveresk
East Lothian	Tyninghame House, Dunbar
Edinburgh & W. Lothian	Dean Gardens & Ann Street
Edinburgh & W. Lothian	61 Fountainhall Road, Edinburgh
Glasgow & District	Kilsyth Gardens
Midlothian	Newhall, Carlops
Perth & Kinross	Glendoick, by Perth
Renfrew & Inverclyde	Duchal, Kilmacolm
Ross, Cromarty, Skye & Inverness	The Hydroponicum, Achiltibuie
Stewartry of Kircudbright	Stockerton, Kircudbright
Stirling	Kilbryde Castle, Dunblane
Wigtown	Woodfall Gardens, Glasserton

Friday 20 May

Fife	Birkhill, near Gauldry

Saturday 21 May

East Lothian	Humbie House, Humbie

Sunday 22 May

Ayrshire	Knockdolian, Colmonell
Berwickshire	Charterhall, Duns
Dumfries	Dabton, Thornhill
Dunbartonshire West	Ross Priory, Gartocharn
Fife	Kirklands, Saline
Lochaber, Badenoch & Strathspey	Ard-Daraich, Ardgour
Perth & Kinross	Fingask Castle, Rait
Stirling	Blairuskin Lodge, Kinlochard
Stirling	Gargunnock House, Gargunnock
Wigtown	Damnaglaur House, Drummore

Friday 27 May

Tweeddale .... Stobo Water Garden, Stobo

Saturday 28 May

Argyll .... Strachur House Woodland Garden
Ayrshire .... Doonholm, Alloway
Caithness,Sutherland&Orkney .... Amat, Ardgay
Edinburgh & W. Lothian .... Dr Neil's Garden, Duddingston
Ross, Cromarty, Skye & Inverness ..... Tullich, Strathcarron

Sunday 29 May

Angus .... Dalfruin, Kirriemuir
Argyll .... Strachur House Woodland Garden
Ayrshire .... Borlandhills, Dunlop
Caithness,Sutherland&Orkney .... Amat, Ardgay
East Lothian .... Inwood, Carberry
Edinburgh & W. Lothian .... Dr Neil's Garden, Duddingston
Edinburgh & W. Lothian .... Suntrap Horticultural Centre
Fife .... Gorno Grove House, by Strathmiglo
Glasgow & District .... 44 Gordon Road, Netherlee
Lochaber,Badenoch&Strathspey .... Aberarder, Kinlochlaggan
Lochaber,Badenoch&Strathspey .... Ardverikie, Kinlochlaggan
Perth & Kinross .... Delvine, Spittalfield
Stewartry of Kircudbright .... Corsock House, Castle Douglas
Stirling .... The Pass House, Kilmahog
Tweeddale .... Hallmanor, Peebles
Wigtown .... Logan Botanic Garden, Port Logan

Monday 30 May

Midlothian .... Cakemuir Castle, Tynehead

Wednesday 1 June

Ross,Cromarty,Skye&Inverness .... House of Gruinard, by Laide

Saturday 4 June

Kincardine & Deeside .... Inchmarlo House Garden, Banchory
Ross,Cromarty,Skye&Inverness .... Attadale, Strathcarron

Sunday 5 June

Aberdeen .... Dunecht House Gardens, Dunecht
Aberdeen .... Gregellen, Banchory Devenick

Aberdeen	Kildrummy Castle Gardens, Alford
Aberdeen	Tillypronie, Tarland
Angus	Cortachy Castle, Kirriemuir
Ayrshire	Barnweil, Craigie
Dumfries	Dalton Burn, Dalton, Lockerbie
Edinburgh & W. Lothian	Kirknewton House, Kirknewton
Glasgow & District	Killorn, Milngavie
Kincardine & Deeside	The Burn House, Glenesk
Midlothian	Penicuik House, Penicuik
Moray & Nairn	Dallas Lodge, Dallas
Perth & Kinross	Meikleour House, by Blairgowrie
Renfrew & Inverclyde	Carruth, Bridge of Weir
Stewartry of Kircudbright	Cally Gardens, Gatehouse of Fleet
Stirling	14 Glebe Crescent, Tillicoultry
Stirling	Lochdochart, Crianlarich

Wednesday 8 June

Ross, Cromarty, Skye & Inverness	Dundonnell House, Dundonnell, by Garve

Saturday 11 June

Argyll	Crarae Garden, Inveraray
Edinburgh & W. Lothian	Sawmill, Harburn
Glasgow & District	Glasgow Botanic Gardens
Midlothian	The Old Sun Inn, & Riga Studio Cottage, Newbattle

Sunday 12 June

Aberdeen	Esslemont, Ellon
Argyll	Crarae Garden, Inveraray
Clydesdale	Biggar Park, Biggar
East Lothian	Gifford Bank with Broadwoodside
Edinburgh & W. Lothian	61 Fountainhall Road, Edinburgh
Fife	Freuchie Plant Sale
Moray & Nairn	Carestown Steading, Deskford
Moray & Nairn	Glen Grant Distillery Garden, Rothes
Perth & Kinross	Balnakeilly, Pitlochry
Ross, Cromarty, Skye & Inverness	Allangrange, Munlochy
Roxburgh	Monteviot, Jedburgh
Stewartry of Kircudbright	The Old Manse, Crossmichael
Stewartry of Kircudbright	19 Rhonepark Crescent, Crossmichael
Tweeddale	Baddinsgill, West Linton
Tweeddale	Broughton Place Stable Cottages, Broughton

Saturday 18 June
Argyll .... Achnacille, Kilmelford
Midlothian .... Lasswade: 16 Kevock Road

Sunday 19 June
Aberdeen .... Howemill, Craigievar, Alford
Argyll .... Achnacille, Kilmelford
Clydesdale .... Dippoolbank Cottage, Carnwath
Fife .... Aytounhill House, Newburgh
Fife .... Culross Village Gardens
Midlothian .... Lasswade: 16 Kevock Road
Moray & Nairn .... Bents Green, 10 Pilmuir Road West, Forres
Perth & Kinross   Explorers, The Scottish Plant Hunters Garden, Pitlochry
Perth & Kinross .... Murthly Castle, by Dunkeld
Renfrew & Inverclyde .... Uplawmoor Village Gardens
Stirling .... Kilbryde Castle, Dunblane

Friday 24 June
Fife .... Kellie Castle, Pittenweem

Saturday 25 June
Caithness, Sutherland & Orkney .... Dunrobin Castle, Golspie

Sunday 26 June
Aberdeen .... Ploughmans Hall, Old Rayne
Caithness, Sutherland & Orkney .... Sandside House, Reay
Clydesdale .... Baitlaws, Lamingoton
Dumfries .... Cowhill Tower, Holywood
East Lothian .... Tyninghame House, Dunbar
Edinburgh & W. Lothian .... Riccarton Mains Farmhouse, Currie
Fife .... Earlshall Castle, Leuchars
Isle of Arran .... Dougarie
Kincardine & Deeside .... Crathes Castle, Banchory
Moray & Nairn .... Gordonstoun, Duffus nr. Elgin
Perth & Kinross .... Annat Lodge, Perth
Roxburgh .... Smailholm Village Gardens
Stewartry of Kircudbright .... Southwick House, Dumfries
Stirling .... Thorntree, Arnprior
Wigtown .... Damnaglaur House, Drummore

Friday 1 July
Fife .... Myres Castle, by Auchtermuchty
Saturday 2 July
Argyll .... Strachur House Woodland Garden

Sunday 3 July
Angus .... Edzell Village
Argyll .... Strachur House Woodland Garden
Berwickshire .... Antons Hill, Coldstream
Fife .... Arnot Tower & Greenhead of Arnot
Kincardine & Deeside .... Drum Castle, Drumoak
Perth & Kinross .... Strathgarry House, Killiecrankie
Ross, Cromarty, Skye & Inverness .... Kilcoy Castle, Muir of Ord
Roxburgh .... Bracken Brae, Linton Downs, Kelso
Roxburgh .... Linton Bankhead Cottage, Morebattle
Roxburgh .... Meadowfield, Old Graden, Kelso
Stewartry of Kircudbright .... Hensol, Mossdale
Wigtown .... Woodfall Gardens, Glasserton

Saturday 9 July
Ayrshire .... Ladyburn, By Maybole
Midlothian .... Barondale House, Riga Studio & The Old Sun Inn,
                                              Newbattle
Roxburgh .... Rose Cottage, Eildon

Sunday 10 July
Aberdeen .... 23 Don Street, Old Aberdeen
Angus .... Gallery, Montrose
Caithness, Sutherland & Orkney .... Kierfiold House, Orkney
Clydesdale .... Carmichael Mill, Hyndford Bridge
Dumfries .... Skairfield, Hightae
Edinburgh .... 36 Morningside Drive, Edinburgh
Fife .... Wormistoune, Crail
Kincardine & Deeside .... Findrack, Torphins
Midlothian .... Barondale House Newbattle
Perth & Kinross .... Campsie Hill, Guildtown
Renfrew & Inverclyde .... Johnstone Gardens
Ross, Cromarty, Skye & Inverness .... Novar, Evanton
Roxburgh .... Rose Cottage, Eildon
Stewartry of Kircudbright .... Burnfoot, Borgue

Wednesday 13 July

Caithness, Sutherland & Orkney .... Castle of Mey, Caithness

Saturday 16 July

Isle of Arran .... Brodick Castle & Country Park

Sunday 17 July

Angus .... Glamis Castle, Glamis
Ayrshire .... Ladyburn, By Maybole
Ayrshire .... Penkill Castle, near Girvan
Berwickshire .... Netherbyres, Eyemouth
Clydesdale .... Biggar Park, Biggar
East Lothian .... Gateside House, Gullane
Edinburgh & W. Lothian .... Lymphoy House, Currie
Ettrick & Lauderdale .... Crosslee Old Farmhouse, Ettrick Valley
Perth & Kinross   Strathtay Gardens, (Pitnacree House &
                                        Cloichfoldich)
Roxburgh .... West Leas, Bonchester Bridge
Stewartry of Kircudbright .... Millhouse, Rhonehouse
Stewartry of Kircudbright .... The Mill House, Gelston

Thursday 21 July

Caithness, Sutherland & OrkneyCastle of Mey, Caithness

Saturday 23 July

Ettrick & Lauderdale .... Carolside, Earlston
Fife .... Crail Small Gardens

Sunday 24 July

Aberdeen .... Leith Hall, Kennethmont
Angus .... The Craig, Montrose
Argyll .... Ardchattan Priory Fete, Connel
Ayrshire .... Carnell, Hurlford
Clydesdale .... Dippoolbank Cottage, Carnwath
Edinburgh & W. Lothian .... 9 Braid Farm Road, Edinburgh
Fife .... Wormistoune, Crail
Kincardine & Deeside .... Douneside House, Tarland
Moray & Nairn .... Knocknagore, Knockando
Perth & Kinross .... Auchleeks, Trinafour
Stewartry of Kircudbright .... Threave Garden, Castle Douglas
Tweeddale .... West Linton Village Gardens

Saturday 30 July

Caithness, Sutherland & Orkney House of Tongue, Tongue

Sunday 31 July

Ayrshire .... Skeldon, Dalrymple
Dumfries .... Hallguards Riverside, Hoddam
Edinburgh & W. Lothian .... Annet House, Linlithgow
Fife .... Earlshall Castle, Leuchars
Glasgow & District .... 35 Montgomerie Street, Eaglesham
Perth & Kinross .... Glenlyon House, Fortingall
Perth & Kinross .... Holestone Lodge, Pool 0' Muckhart
Renfrew & Inverclyde .... Kilmacolm
Ross, Cromarty, Skye & Inverness Glen Kyllachy, Tomatin
Stewartry of Kircudbright .... Arndarroch Cottage, St John's Town of Dalry
Tweeddale .... Portmore, Eddleston

Sunday 7 August

Ayrshire .... Blairquhan, Straiton, Maybole
Caithness, Sutherland & Orkney .... Langwell, Berriedale
Fife .... West Kincaple House, by St Andrews
Fife .... Ladies Lake, St Andrews
Glasgow & District .... The Gardens of St Leonards, East Kilbride
Kincardine & Deeside .... Glenbervie House, Drumlithie
Moray & Nairn .... Bents Green, 10 Pilmuir Road West, Forres
Perth & Kinross .... Cluniemore, Pitlochry
Perth & Kinross .... Drummond Castle Gardens, Muthill
Renfrew & Inverclyde .... Barshaw Park, Paisley
Ross, Cromarty, Skye & Inverness House of Aigas & Field Centre, Beauly
Roxburgh .... Yetholm Village
Stewartry of Kircudbright .... Crossmichael Gardens, Castle Douglas

Saturday 13 August

Isle of Arran .... Brodick Castle & Country Park

Sunday 14 August

Aberdeen .... Castle Fraser, Kemnay
Ayrshire .... Moorholm, Rowallan
Caithness, Sutherland & Orkney .... Langwell, Berriedale
Clydesdale .... Carnwath Village Gardens Trail, Carnwath

Fife .... Saline Village Gardens
Stewartry of Kircudbright .... Cally Gardens, Gatehouse of Fleet
Wigtown .... Craichlaw, Kirkcowan

Sunday 21 August
Edinburgh .... 61 Fountainhall Road, Edinburgh
Fife .... Falkland Palace Garden
Stewartry of Kircudbright .... Crofts, Kirkpatrick Durham

Sunday 28 August
Fife .... Balcarres, Colinsburgh

Sunday 4 September
Dunbartonshire West .... Hill House Plant Sale, Helensburgh
Tweeddale .... Broughton Place Stable Cottages, Broughton
Tweeddale .... Dawyck Botanic Garden, Stobo

Sunday 11 September
Fife .... 3 Small Gardens - St Andrews
Renfrew & Inverclyde .... SGS Plant Sale, Finlaystone, Langbank
Ross, Cromarty, Skye & Inverness Inverewe, Poolewe

Sunday 18 September
Fife .... Cambo House, Kingsbarns
Perth & Kinross .... Explorers, The Scottish Plant Hunters Garden,
                                                        Pitlochry

Saturday 24 September
Edinburgh & W. Lothian .... Lothian Plant Sale, Kirknewton House,
                                                        Kirknewton

Saturday 1 October
Fife .... SGS Plant Sale, Hill of Tarvit

Sunday 2 October
Fife .... SGS Plant Sale, Hill of Tarvit

Sunday 9 October
Edinburgh & W. Lothian .... 61 Fountainhall Road, Edinburgh

Saturday 15 October
East & Mid Lothian .... SGS Plant Sale, Dalkeith

Sunday 23 October
Perth & Kinross .... Stobhall, by Perth

PLANT SALES 2005
See District Lists for further details

<u>Renfrew & Inverclyde</u>
Carruth, Bridge of Weir
Sunday 5 June 2 - 5pm

<u>Glasgow & District</u>
Glasgow Botanic Gardens
Saturday 11 June 11am - 4pm

<u>Fife</u>
Freuchie Plant Sale
Sunday 12 June Noon - 4pm

<u>Dunbartonshire West</u>
Hill House, Helensburgh
Sunday 4 September 11am - 4pm

<u>Renfrew & Inverclyde</u>
Finlaystone, Langbank
Sunday 11 September 11.30am - 4pm

<u>Edinburgh & West Lothian</u>
Kirknewton House, Kirknewton
Saturday 24 September 11.30am - 4pm

<u>Fife</u>
Hill of Tarvit, Cupar
Saturday 1 October 10.30 - 4pm & Sunday 2 October 11am - 4pm

<u>East & Midlothian</u>
Oxenfoord Mains, Dalkeith
Saturday 15 October 9.30 am- 3.30pm

ABERDEEN

District Organiser	**Mrs J Pilc**, 15 South Avenue, Cults, Aberdeen AB15 9LQ,
Area Organisers:	**Mrs S Callen,** Cults House, Cults Avenue, Aberdeen AB15 9TB
	Mrs F G Lawson, Asloun, Alford AB33 8NR
	Mrs A Robertson, Drumblade House, Huntly AB54 6ER
	Mrs F M K Tuck, Allargue House, Corgarff AB36 8YP
Hon. Treasurer:	**Mr J Ludlow**. St Nicholas House, Banchory AB31 5YT

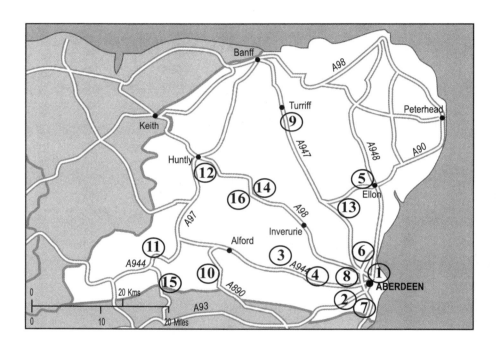

DATES OF OPENING

Blairwood, Aberdeen .... June – October by appointment
23 Don Street, Old Aberdeen .... June – August by appointment
Grandhome, Aberdeen .... By appointment
Greenridge, Cults .... July & August by appointment
Hatton Castle, Turriff .... By appointment
Howemill, Craigievar .... By appointment
Ploughman's Hall, Old Rayne .... By appointment
Waterside Farmhouse, Oyne .... By appointment

Dunecht House Gardens, Dunecht	Sunday 5 June	1 - 5pm
Gregellen, Banchory Devenick	Sunday 5 June	2 - 5pm
Kildrummy Castle Gardens, Alford	Sunday 5 June	10am - 5pm
Tillypronie, Tarland	Sunday 5 June	2 - 5pm
Esslemont, Ellon	Sunday 12 June	1 - 4.30pm
Howemill, Craigievar, Alford	Sunday 19 June	1.30 - 5pm
Ploughmans Hall, Old Rayne	Sunday 26 June	1 - 6pm
23 Don Street, Old Aberdeen	Sunday 10 July	1.30 - 6pm
Leith Hall, Kennethmont	Sunday 24 July	Noon - 5pm
Castle Fraser, Kemnay	Sunday 14 August	1 - 5pm
Waterside Farmhouse, Oyne	Sunday 21 August	1 - 5pm
Tillypronie, Tarland	Sunday 28 August	2 - 5pm
Pitmedden Garden, Ellon	Sunday 28 August	1 - 5pm

1. 23 DON STREET, Old Aberdeen ♿

(Miss M & Mr G Mackechnie)

Atmospheric walled garden in historic Old Aberdeen. Wide range of rare and unusual plants and old-fashioned scented roses. Full afternoon tea £2.00. Plant stall. Park at St Machar Cathedral, short walk down Chanonry to Don Street, turn right. City plan ref: P7.

Admission £2.00 Concessions £1.50

OPEN JUNE TO AUGUST BY APPOINTMENT Tel: 01224 487269.

SUNDAY 10 JULY 1.30 - 6pm

40% to Cat Protection 60% net to SGS Charities

✻ 2. BLAIRWOOD HOUSE, South Deeside Road, Blairs

(Ilse Elders)

Approximately a half acre country garden. Most of it started from scratch five years ago and still evolving. The garden has been self-designed to provide colour over a long season, without requiring daily care from the owner. Herbaceous borders, small beautiful herb garden packed with well over a hundred medicinal and culinary herbs, pebble mosaics and sunken patio area. (Very close to Blairs Museum) Teas and coffees available at Ardroe Hotel or The Old Mill Inn, just down the road. Route: Blairs, on the B9077, 5 mins by car from Bridge of Dee, Aberdeen.

BY APPOINTMENT MID JUNE to BEGINNING OF OCTOBER Tel: 01224 868301

40% to Aberdeen Greenbelt Alliance 60% net to SGS Charities

3. CASTLE FRASER, Kemnay ♿

(The National Trust for Scotland)

Castle Fraser, one of the most spectacular of the Castles of Mar, built between 1575 and 1635 with designed landscape and parkland the work of Thomas White 1794. Includes an exciting new garden development within the traditional walled garden of cut flowers, trees, shrubs and new herbaceous borders. Also a medicinal and culinary border, organically grown fruit and vegetables and a newly constructed woodland garden with adventure playground. Plant and produce sales and home baked teas. Near Kemnay, off A944.

Admission £2.00 Children & NTS members £1.00

SUNDAY 14 AUGUST 1 - 5pm

40% to The Gardens Fund of The National Trust for Scotland 60% net to SGS Charities

For other opening details see NTS advert at the back of the book

4. DUNECHT HOUSE GARDENS, Dunecht   ♿ (partly)

(The Hon. Charles A Pearson)
A magnificent copper beech avenue leads to Dunecht House built by John and William Smith with a Romanesque addition in 1877 by G Edmund Street. Highlights include rhododendrons, azaleas and a wildflower garden. Teas. Cars free. Dunecht 1 mile, routes: A944 and B977.
Admission £3.00 Concessions £1.50
SUNDAY 5 JUNE 1 - 5pm
40% to Riding for the Disabled 60% net to SGS Charities

---

5. ESSLEMONT, Ellon

(Mr & Mrs Wolrige Gordon of Esslemont)
Victorian house set in wooded policies above River Ythan. Roses and shrubs in garden with double yew hedges (17th and 18th centuries). Music, stalls, charity stalls, tombola. Home baked teas. Ellon 2 miles. Route: A920 from Ellon. On Pitmedden/Oldmeldrum Road.
Admission: £2.00 Children (4 – 11 years) & Concessions £1.00
SUNDAY 12 JUNE 1 - 4.30pm
40% to Conerstone Community Care 60% net to SGS Charities

---

6. GRANDHOME, Aberdeen   ♿

(Mr & Mrs D R Paton)
18th century walled garden, incorporating rose garden; policies with rhododendrons, azaleas, mature trees and shrubs. Depending on the time of year, plants, fruit or vegetables may be available to buy. Route: from north end of North Anderson Drive, continue on A90 over Persley Bridge, turning left at Tesco roundabout. No dogs please.
Admission £2.50 Teas by arrangement
OPEN BY APPOINTMENT Tel: 01224 722 202
40% to Children First 60% net to SGS Charities

✿7. GREGELLEN HOUSE, Banchory Devenick, Aberdeenshire

(Mr & Mrs McGregor)
Former Victorian manse set in 1½ acres of garden. Herbaceous borders, lawns and rockeries with a wide and varied range of interesting plants which include azaleas, meconopsis, peonies and rhododendrons, making a colourful display. Teas and plant stall. Route: Approximately 1 - ¾ of a mile from bridge of Dee off the B9077 South Deeside road.
Admission: £2.50 Children 50p
SUNDAY 5 JUNE 2-5pm
40% to Marie Curie Cancer Care 60% net to SGS Charities

---

8. GREENRIDGE, Craigton Road, Cults

(BP Exploration)
Large secluded garden surrounding 1840 Archibald Simpson house, for many years winner of Britain in Bloom 'Best Hidden Garden'. Mature specimen trees and shrubs. Sloping walled rose garden and terraces. Kitchen garden. Teas. Plant stall. Route: directions with booking.
Admission £3.50 including tea
JULY & AUGUST BY APPOINTMENT. Tel: 01224 860200 Fax: 01224 860210
40% to Association of the Friends of Raeden 60% net to SGS Charities

9. HATTON CASTLE, Turriff   ♿ with help
(Mr & Mrs James Duff)
Two acre walled garden featuring mixed borders and shrub roses with yew and box hedges and allees of pleached hornbeam. Kitchen garden and fan trained fruit trees. Lake and woodland walks. Afternoon tea and lunch parties by appointment. On A947 2 miles south of Turriff. Admission £4.50 Children free
OPEN BY APPOINTMENT
Tel: 01888 562279 Fax: 01888 563943 Email - *jjdgardens@btinternet.com*
40% to Future Hope 60% net to SGS Charities

10. HOWEMILL, Craigievar   ♿ with help
(Mr D Atkinson)
Expanding garden with a wide range of unusual alpines, shrubs and herbaceous plants. Plant stall. Teas. From Alford take A980 Alford/Lumphanan road. No dogs please. Admission £2.00 Children under 12 free
Sunday 19 June 1.30 - 5pm or by appointment. Tel: 01975 581278.
40% to Cancer Relief Macmillan Fund 60% net to SGS Charities

11. KILDRUMMY CASTLE GARDENS, Alford   ♿ (with help)
(Kildrummy Garden Trust)
April shows the gold of the lysichitons in the water garden, and the small bulbs naturalised beside the copy of the 14th century Brig o' Balgownie. Rhododendrons and azaleas from April (frost permitting). September/October brings colchicums and brilliant colour with acers, fothergillas and viburnums. Plants for sale. Play area. Tea room. Wheelchair facilities. Car park free inside hotel main entrance. Coach park up hotel delivery entrance. Parties by arrangement. *www.kildrummy-castle-gardens.co.uk* Open daily April - October. Tel: 01975 571277/571203. On A97, 10 miles from Alford, 17 miles from Huntly.
Admission £3.00 Children free
SUNDAY 5 JUNE 10am - 5pm
40% to Marie Curie Cancer Care 60% net to SGS Charities

12. LEITH HALL, Kennethmont
(The National Trust for Scotland)
This attractive old country house, the earliest part of which dates from 1650, was the home of the Leith and Leith-Hay families for more than three centuries. The west garden was made by Mr and The Hon. Mrs Charles Leith-Hay around the beginning of the twentieth century. The property was given to the Trust in 1945. The rock garden has been enhanced by the Scottish Rock Garden Club in celebration of their 150th anniversary. Toilet for disabled visitors. Cream teas. Pipe band. Plant sales. Walks with the Head Gardener. On B9002 near Kennethmont. Plants for sale.
Admission House - £7.00 Concs & Children £5.25 Garden - £2.50 Concs & Children £1.90
SUNDAY 24 JULY Noon - 5pm
40% to The Gardens Fund of The National Trust for Scotland 60% net to SGS Charities

13. PITMEDDEN GARDEN, Ellon &

(The National Trust for Scotland)
Garden created by Lord Pitmedden in 1675. Elaborate floral designs in parterres of box edging, inspired by the garden at the Palace of Holyroodhouse, have been re-created by the Trust. Fountains and sundials make fine centrepieces to the garden, filled in summer with 60,000 annual flowers. Also herb garden, herbaceous borders, trained fruit, plant sales, Museum of Farming Life, Visitor Centre, nature hut, woodland walk and wildlife garden. Tearoom. Special rates for pre-booked coach parties.
Admission £5.00 Concessions & children £4.00
SUNDAY 28 AUGUST 1 - 5pm
40% to The Gardens Fund of The National Trust for Scotland 60% net to SGS Charities

14. PLOUGHMAN'S HALL, Old Rayne & with help

(Mr & Mrs A Gardner)
One acre garden. Rock, herbaceous, kitchen, herb and woodland gardens. Plant and craft stalls. Off A96, 9 miles north of Inverurie.
Admission £2.00 Children 50p
SUNDAY 26 JUNE 1 - 6pm also open by appointment Tel: 01464 851253
40% to Wycliffe Bible Translators 60% net to SGS Charities

15. TILLYPRONIE, Tarland &

(The Hon Philip Astor)
Late Victorian house for which Queen Victoria laid foundation stone. Herbaceous borders, terraced garden, heather beds, water garden and new rockery. New Golden Jubilee garden still being laid out. Shrubs and ornamental trees, including pinetum with rare specimens. Fruit garden and greenhouses. Superb views. Home-made teas. Plant sale - June opening only. Free car park. Dogs on lead, please. Between Ballater and Strathdon, off A97.
Admission £2.00 Children £1.00
SUNDAY 5 JUNE 2 - 5pm - Wonderful show of azaleas and spring heathers
SUNDAY 28 AUGUST 2 - 5pm
All proceeds to Scotland's Gardens Scheme

16. WATERSIDE FARMHOUSE, Oyne

(Ann & Colin Millar)
A garden, started in 1991 from a rough farmyard. Maturing woodland extends to 2 acres around 19th century farmhouse and courtyard with cordoned fruit trees orchard and kitchen garden. Mixed shrub and herbaceous borders, pond, heathers and herbs, to give interest year round. Tea and biscuits. Plants usually available. No dogs please. Off A96, ½ mile north of junction with B9002.
Admission £2.00 Children £1.00
SUNDAY 21 AUGUST 1 - 5pm also open by appointment Tel: 01464 851658
40% to Books Abroad 60% net to SGS Charities

ANGUS

District Organiser: **Mrs Nici Rymer,** Nether Finlarg, Forfar DD8 1XQ

Area Organisers: **Miss Ruth Dundas,** Caddam, Kinnordy, Kirriemuir DD8 4LP
Mrs J Henderson, Mains of Panmuir, by Carnoustie DD7
Mrs R Porter, West Scryne, By Carnoustie DD7 6LL
Mrs C Smoor, Gagie House, Tealing, Dundee DD4 0PR
Mrs A Stormonth Darling, Lednathie, Glen Prosen Kirriemuir
DD8

Hon. Treasurer: **Col R H B Learoyd,** Priestoun, Edzell DD9 7UD

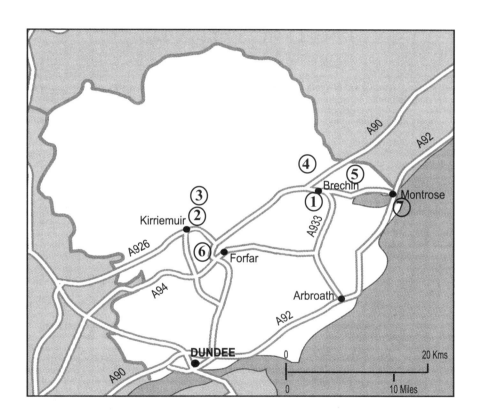

DATES OF OPENING

House of Pitmuies, Guthrie, by Forfar .... 1 April - 31 October   10am - 5pm

Brechin Castle, Brechin	Sunday 15 May	2 - 5.30pm
Dalfruin, Kirriemuir	Sunday 29 May	2 - 5pm
Cortachy Castle, Kirriemuir	Sunday 5 June	2 - 6pm
Edzell Village	Sunday 3 July	2 - 5pm
Gallery, Montrose	Sunday 10 July	2 - 5pm
Glamis Castle, Glamis	Sunday 17 July	10am - 6pm
The Craig House, Montrose	Sunday 24 July	2 - 5.30pm

1. BRECHIN CASTLE, Brechin
(The Earl & Countess of Dalhousie)
Ancient fortress of Scottish kings on cliff overlooking River Southesk. Rebuilt by Alexander Edward – completed in 1711. Extensive walled garden 300 yards from Castle with ancient and new plantings and mown lawn approach. Rhododendrons, azaleas, bulbs, interesting trees, wild garden. Tea in garden. Car parking free. Route: A90, Brechin 1 mile.
Admission £2.50 Children 50p
SUNDAY 15 MAY 2 - 5.30pm
20% to Dalhousie Day Centre   20% to Unicorn Preservation Society   60% net to SGS Charities

2. CORTACHY CASTLE, Kirriemuir
(The Earl & Countess of Airlie)
16th century castellated house. Additions in 1872 by David Bryce. Spring garden and wild pond garden with azaleas, primroses and rhododendrons. Garden of fine American specie trees and river walk along South Esk. Teas. Plant sale and plant raffle, children's quiz, Aberdeen Angus organic beef for sale.
Kirriemuir 5 miles. Route B955.
Admission £2.50 Children 50p
SUNDAY 5 JUNE 2 - 6pm
20% to Kirriemuir Day Care Minibus Appeal   20% Hospitalfield House, Arbroath
60% net to SGS Charities

3. DALFRUIN, Kirktonhill Road, Kirriemuir   ♿ (with assistance – grass paths just wide enough)
(Mr & Mrs James A Welsh)
A well-stocked mature garden of almost one-third of an acre situated at end of cul-de-sac. Unusual plants, dactylorhiza, tree peonies, meconopsis, trilliums. Stream added in Autumn 2000 (Newts first seen autumn 2003!). Good plant stall. No dogs please. Unless disabled please park on Roods or at St Mary's Church. From centre of Kirriemuir turn left up Roods; Kirktonhill Road is on left near top of hill, just before the school 20 mph zone.
Admission £2.50 Accompanied children free Teas at St Mary's Church. Plant stall.
SUNDAY 29 MAY 2 - 5pm
20% to The Glens & Kirriemuir Old Parish Church   20% St Mary's Scottish Episcopal Church
60% net to SGS Charities

4. EDZELL VILLAGE

Walk round 10 gardens in Edzell village. Teas extra. Tickets are on sale in the village and a plan is issued with the tickets.

Admission £2.50 Children 50p

SUNDAY 3 JULY 2 - 5pm

40% to Cancer Research UK 60% net to SGS Charities

5. GALLERY, Montrose

(Mr & Mrs John Simson)

Redesign and replanting of this historic garden have preserved and extended its traditional framework of holly, privet and box. A grassed central alley, embellished with circles, links interesting theme gardens and lawns. A short walk leads to the raised bank of the North River Esk with views towards the Howe of the Mearns. From that point rough paths lead west and east along the bank. Route: From A90 immediately south of Northwater Bridge take exit to 'Hillside' and next left to 'Gallery & Marykirk'. Or from A937 immediately west of of rail underpass follow signs to 'Gallery & Northwater Bridge'.

Admission £2.50 Children 50p

SUNDAY 10 JULY 2 - 5pm

40% to Intermediate Technology Development Group 60% net to SGS Charities

6. GLAMIS CASTLE, Glamis ♿

(The Earl of Strathmore & Kinghorne)

Family home of the Earls of Strathmore and a royal residence since 1372. Childhood home of HM Queen Elizabeth The Queen Mother, birthplace of HRH The Princess Margaret, and legendary setting for Shakespeare's play 'Macbeth'. Five-storey L-shaped tower block dating from 15th century, remodelled 1600, containing magnificent rooms with wide range of historic pictures, furniture, porcelain etc. Spacious grounds with river and woodland walks through pinetum and nature trail. Walled garden exhibition. Formal garden. For this day only the greenhouses and famous vine collection will be open. Restaurant. Teas. Shopping pavilion. Glamis 1 mile A94.

Admission to Castle & grounds: £7.00, OAPs £5.70, children £3.80.

Admission: Grounds only £3.50 Children & OAPs £2.50

SUNDAY 17 JULY 10am - 6pm

40% to Princess Royal Trust for Carers 60% net to SGS Charities

7. HOUSE OF PITMUIES, Guthrie, By Forfar

(Mrs Farquhar Ogilvie)

Two semi-formal wall gardens adjoin 18th century house and shelter long borders of herbaceous perennials, superb delphiniums, old fashioned roses and pavings with violas and dianthus. Spacious lawns, river and lochside walks beneath fine trees. A wide variety of shrubs with good autumn colours. Massed spring bulbs, interesting turreted doocot and "Gothick" wash-house. Dogs on lead please. Rare and unusual plants for sale. Fruit in season. Friockheim 1½ miles Route A932.

Admission £2.50

1 APRIL - 31 OCTOBER 10am - 5pm

Donation to Scotland's Gardens Scheme

8. THE CRAIG, Montrose

(Mr and Mrs J F Horn)

Fifteenth century house overlooking Montrose Basin, surrounded by newly planted walled gardens. Herbaceous, roses, annuals, herb garden and orchard. Teas. Dogs on lead please. Half mile south of Montrose, off A92.

Admission £2.50 Children 60p

SUNDAY 24 JULY 2 – 5.30pm

40% to Scottish Wildlife Trust   60% net to SGS Charities

ARGYLL

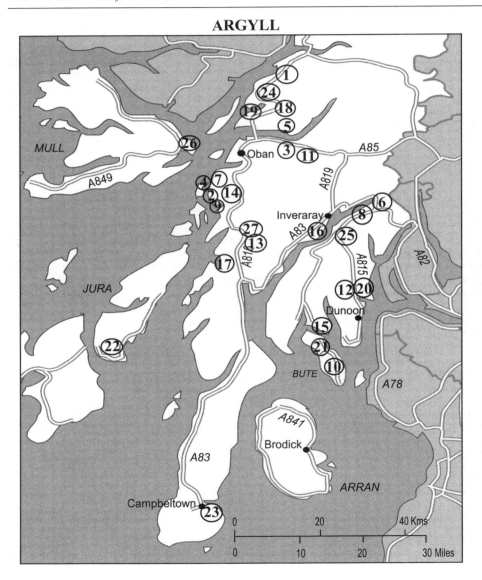

District Organiser   **Mrs C Struthers,** Ardmaddy Castle, Balvicar PA34 4QY
& Hon Treasurer:

Area Organisers:
      Mrs G Cadzow, Duachy, Kilninver, Oban PA34 4RH
      Mrs E B Ingleby, Braighbhaille, Crarae, Inveraray PA32 8YA
      Mrs P Lang, Ardrannoch,Ledaig PA37 1QU
      Mrs A Staunton, Ardare, Colintraive PA22 3AS

DATES OF OPENING

Achnacloich, Connel	Daily 25 March - 31 October	10am - 6pm
An Cala, Ellenabeich	Daily 1 April - 31 October	10am - 6pm
Ardchattan Priory, North Connel.	Daily 1 April - 31 October	9am - 6pm
Ardkinglas Woodland Garden	Daily all year round	daylight hours
Ardmaddy Castle, by Oban	Daily all year	9am - sunset
Ardno, Cairndow	By appointment	
Ascog Hall, Isle of Bute	Daily (except Mons & Tues)	
	Easter - End October	10am - 5pm
Barguillean's "Angus Garden"	Daily all year	9am - 6pm
Cnoc-na-Garrie, Ballymeanoch	Daily 25 Mar - 31 Oct	
	(Closed Mon & Tues)	10am - 6pm
Coille Dharaich Kilmelford	By appt most days 15 April - 15 Sept	
Druimavuic House, Appin	Daily April, May & June	10am - 6pm
Druimneil House, Port Appin	Daily 1 April - 31 October	9am - 6pm
Eckford, By Dunoon	Daily 9 April - 6 June	10am - 5pm
Glecknabae, Isle of Bute	By appointment Spring - Autumn	
Jura House, Ardfin, Isle of Jura.	Open all year	9am - 5pm
Kildalloig, Campbeltown	By appointment	
Kinlochlaich House Gardens, Appin.	Open all year	9.30 -5.30 or dusk
	Except Suns Oct - Mar Suns Apr - Sept 10.30am - 5.30pm	
Torosay Castle Gardens, Isle of Mull	Gardens open all year	
26 Kilmartin, Lochgilphead	1 June - 30 Sept Mon & Thurs & by appt.	
	10.30am - Dusk	

Benmore Botanic Garden, Dunoon	Sunday 24 April	10am - 6pm
Strachur House Woodland Garden	Sat & Sun 30 Apr & 1 May	1 - 5pm
Crinan Hotel Garden, Crinan	Saturday 7 May	Noon - 5pm
Arduaine, Kilmelford	Sat & Sun 7 & 8 May	9.30 - 6pm
Colintraive Gardens .	Sat & Sun 14 & 15 May	1 - 5pm
Achara House, Duror of Appin	Sunday 15 May	2 - 6pm
Strachur House Woodland Garden	Sat & Sun 28 & 29 May	1 - 5pm
Crarae Glen Garden, Inveraray	Sat & Sun 11 & 12 June	9.30am - 6pm
Achnacille, Kilmelford	Sat & Sun 18 &19 June	2 - 6pm
Strachur House Woodland Garden	Sat & Sun 2 & 3 July	1- 5pm
Glecknabae, Rothesay, Isle of Bute	Sunday 3 July	10.30am - 4.30pm
Ardchattan Priory Fete, Connel	Sunday 24 July	Noon - 4pm

1. ACHARA HOUSE, Duror of Appin &

(Mr & Mrs Alastair Macpherson of Pitmain)
A recently created garden set round the attractive Achara House (attributed to Robert Lorimer), containing an extensive collection of rhododendron species and hybrids, azaleas and camellias. Hill garden with fine view of Loch Linnhe. Teas. On A828 just south of Duror, 7 miles south of Ballachulish Bridge and 5 miles north of Appin.
Admission £2.00 Children free
SUNDAY 15 MAY 2 - 6pm
40% to Cancer Relief Macmillan Fund 60% net to SGS Charities

2. ACHNACILLE, Kilmelford, by Oban

(Mr & Mrs Robin Asbury)
Created from a hillside a few years ago, a one acre garden at the head of Loch Melfort with sweeping views down the Loch.   Varied plantings of trees, shrubs and herbaceous. Pond and streamside plants and a small rock garden. Teas. Plant stall. Route: ½ a mile from Kilmelford (A816) on road signposted 'Degnish'
Admission £2.00 Children Free
SATURDAY & SUNDAY 18 & 19 JUNE 2 - 6pm
40% to Kilmelford Parish Church 60% net to SGS Charities

3. ACHNACLOICH, Connel &

(Mrs T E Nelson)
Scottish baronial house by John Starforth of Glasgow. Succession of bulbs, flowering shrubs, rhododendrons, azaleas, magnolias and primulas. Woodland garden with ponds above Loch Etive. Good Autumn colours. Plants for sale.   Dogs on lead please. On the A85 3 miles east of Connel.
Admission £2.00   Children free OAPs £1.00
DAILY 25 MARCH - 31 OCTOBER 10am - 6pm
All takings to Scotland's Gardens Scheme

4. AN CALA, Ellenabeich, Isle of Seil

(Mrs Thomas Downie)
A small garden of under five acres designed in the 1930s, An Cala sits snugly in its horse-shoe shelter of surrounding cliffs. A very pretty garden with streams, waterfall, ponds, many herbaceous plants as well as azaleas, rhododendrons and cherry trees in spring. Proceed south from Oban on Campbeltown road for 8 miles, turn right at Easdale sign, a further 8 miles on B844; garden between school and village.
Admission £2.00 Children free
DAILY FROM 1 APRIL - 31 OCTOBER 10am - 6pm
Donation to Scotland's Gardens Scheme

5. ARDCHATTAN PRIORY, North Connel ♿

(Mrs Sarah Troughton)
Beautifully situated on the north side of Loch Etive. The Priory, founded in 1230, is now a private house. The ruins of the chapel and graveyard, with fine early stones, are in the care of Historic Scotland and open with the garden. The front of the house has a rockery, extensive herbaceous and rose borders, with excellent views over Loch Etive. To the west of the house there are shrub borders and a wild garden, numerous roses and over 30 different varieties of Sorbus providing excellent autumn colour. Oban 10 miles. From north, turn left off A828 at Barcaldine on to B845 for 6 miles. From Oban or the east on A85, cross Connel Bridge and turn first right, proceed east on Bonawe Road. Well signed.
Admission £2.50 Children free
DAILY FROM 1 APRIL - 31 OCTOBER 9am - 6pm
A fete will be held on SUNDAY 24 JULY Noon - 4pm
Donation to Scotland's Gardens Scheme

---

6. ARDKINGLAS WOODLAND GARDEN, Cairndow

(Ardkinglas Estate)
In peaceful setting overlooking Loch Fyne the garden contains one of the finest collections of rhododendrons and conifers in Britain. This includes the mightiest conifer in Europe and one of Britain's tallest trees as well as many other champion trees. Gazebo with unique "Scriptorium" based around a collection of literary quotes. Woodland lochan, ancient mill ruins and many woodland walks. Plant and gift sales, picnic facilities, car park and toilets. Dogs allowed on a lead. Entrance through Cairndow village off A83 Loch Lomond/Inveraray road.
Admission £3.00 Children under 16 years free. Scottish Tourist Board 3* Garden.
OPEN DAYLIGHT HOURS ALL YEAR ROUND
Donation to Scotland's Gardens Scheme

---

7. ARDMADDY CASTLE, Balvicar, by Oban ♿ (mostly)

(Mr & Mrs Charles Struthers)
Ardmaddy Castle, with its woodlands and formal walled garden on one side and spectacular views to the islands and the sea on the other, has many fine rhododendrons and azaleas with a variety of trees, shrubs, unusual vegetables and flower borders between dwarf box hedges. Daffodils and bluebell woods. Recently created water gardens and stoneworks add increasing interest to this continuously developing garden. Sales area with many unusual plants and shrubs, and veg and fruit when available. Toilet. Oban 13 miles, Easdale 3 miles. 1½ miles of narrow road off B844 to Easdale.
Admission £2.50 Children 50p
DAILY ALL YEAR 9am - sunset
Other visits by arrangement: Tel. 01852 300353
Donations to Scotland's Gardens Scheme

✿ 8. ARDNO, Cairndow

(Kate How)
Begun in 1992 - an overgrown canvas in need of extensive clearing. 12 years on it is becoming well established with interesting trees and shrubs around the house, through the beautiful wooded gorge and down to the Loch via the meadow/arboretum. The site is stunning and the garden is maturing amazingly quickly. Interesting for those planning to start from scratch! Situated at the top end of Loch Fyne betweeen Cairndow and St Catherines, off the A815.
Admission £2.50 Children free
OPEN BY APPOINTMENT Tel: 01499 302052
40% to S J Noble Trust   60% net to SGS Charities

37

9. ARDUAINE, Kilmelford   ♿

(The National Trust for Scotland)

An outstanding 20 acre coastal garden on the Sound of Jura. Begun more than 100 years ago on the south facing slope of a promontory separating Asknish Bay from Loch Melfort, this remarkable hidden paradise, protected by tall shelterbelts and influenced favourably by the Gulf Stream, grows a wide variety of plants from the four corners of the globe. Internationally known for the rhododendron species collection, the garden also features magnolias, camellias, azaleas and many other wonderful trees and shrubs, many of which are tender and not often seen. A broad selection of perennials, bulbs, ferns and water plants ensure a year-long season of interest. Route: Off the A816 Oban - Lochgilphead, sharing an entrance with the Loch Melfort Hotel. Admission Adults £5.00 Concessions £4.00 Under 5s free Family £14.00

SATURDAY & SUNDAY 7 & 8 MAY 9.30am - 6pm

40% to The Gardens Fund of The National Trust for Scotland   60% net to SGS Charities

---

10. ASCOG HALL, Ascog, Isle of Bute

(Mr & Mrs W Fyfe)

Recently restored after decades of neglect, this appealing garden is continuing to develop and mature, with an abundance of choice plants and shrubs which delight the eye from spring to autumn. It includes a formal rose garden with a profusion of fragrant old shrub roses. Through a rustic ivy-clad stone arch which in bygone years led to the tennis court, there is now a large gravel garden with sun-loving plants and grasses. Undoubtedly, however, the most outstanding feature is our acclaimed Victorian fernery. This rare and beautiful structure houses subtropical and temperate fern species, including an ancient Todea barbara - the only survivor from the original collection, and said to be around 1,000 years old. Plant Stall.
Admission £3.00 Children free, under supervision. Sorry no dogs

OPEN DAILY (Except Mons & Tues) EASTER - END OCTOBER 10am - 5pm

Donation to Scotland's Gardens Scheme

---

11. BARGUILLEAN'S "ANGUS GARDEN", Taynuilt

(Mr Robin Marshall)

Nine acre woodland garden around an eleven acre loch set in the Glen Lonan hills. Spring flowering shrubs and bulbs, extensive collection of rhododendron hybrids, deciduous azaleas, primulas, conifers and unusual trees. The garden contains a large collection of North American rhododendron hybrids from famous comtemporary plant breeders. Some paths can be steep. 3 marked walks from 30 minutes to 1½ hours. Coach tours by arrangement. Contact Sean Honeyman Tel 01866 822 335 Route: 3 miles south off A85 Glasgow/Oban road at Taynuilt; road marked Glen Lonan; 3 miles up single track road; turn right at sign.
Admission £2.00 Children free

DAILY ALL YEAR 9am - 6pm

Donation to Scotland's Gardens Scheme

12. BENMORE BOTANIC GARDEN, Dunoon   ♿ (limited due to hill slopes)

(Regional Garden of the Royal Botanic Garden Edinburgh and one of the National Botanic Gardens of Scotland)

World famous for its magnificent conifers and its extensive range of flowering trees and shrubs, including over 250 species of rhododendron. From a spectacular avenue of Giant Redwoods, numerous waymarked walks lead the visitor via a formal garden and pond through hillside woodlands to a dramatic viewpoint overlooking the Eachaig valley and the Holy Loch. James Duncan Cafe (licensed) and Botanics Shop for gifts and plants. Also newly renovated Courtyard Gallery with events and exhibitions. Dogs permitted on a short leash. 7 miles north of Dunoon or 22 miles south from Glen Kinglass below Rest and Be Thankful pass; on A815.

Admission £3.50 Concessions £3.00 Children £1.00 Families £8.00

SUNDAY 24 APRIL 10am - 6pm

Donation to Scotland's Gardens Scheme
For further details see advert at back of book

---

13. CNOC-NA-GARRIE, Ballymeanoch, by Lochgilphead

(Mrs Dorothy Thomson)

A garden being created from rough hillside, designed for year-round interest. Large range of alpines, shrubs, grasses, herbaceous plants and bulbs, many grown from seed.

Plant stall. 2 miles south of Kilmartin, A816. Entrance sharp left between cottages and red brick house, continue up track to bungalow. No dogs please.

Admission £2.00 Accompanied children free.

OPEN DAILY 25 MARCH - 31 OCTOBER (Closed Mons & Tues) 10am - 6pm

20% to British Red Cross Society (mid Argyll)   20% to Cancer Relief Macmillan Fund
60% net to SGS Charities

---

14. COILLE DHARAICH, Kilmelford, Oban   ♿ (with assistance)

(Drs Alan & Hilary Hill)

This mature small garden is on a raised beach and is centered on a natural rock outcrop and pool. Plants range from alpines in screes and troughs to small herbaceous plants, shrubs, conifers and decidous trees. These plants all survive and some thrive in this wet and windy garden. Suitable for wheelchairs with a strong pusher. Sorry no dogs. Plants for sale. Half a mile from Kilmelford (A816) on road signposted "Degnish".

Admission £2.00 Children Free

OPEN BY APPOINTMENT MOST DAYS
FROM   APRIL TO SEPTEMBER. Tel: 01852 200285

40% to Princess Royal Trust for Carers (N. Argyll Carers Centre) 60% net to SGS Charities

---

15. COLINTRAIVE GARDENS

Three spring and woodland gardens all overlooking the Kyles of Bute in this very beautiful corner of Argyll. They are of varied interest and within easy reach of each other. Home baked teas are available at the Village Hall.

1 - **Breamanach**   Mrs A Neal
2 - **Dunyvaig**   Mrs M Donald
3 - **Caol Ruadh**   Mr & Mrs C Scotland

Tickets and maps obtainable at all gardens. Dogs on a lead please. Route: Off A886, 20 miles from Dunoon

Admission £2.00, includes all 3 gardens. Children free

SATURDAY & SUNDAY 14 & 15 MAY 1 - 5pm

All takings to Scotland's Gardens Scheme.

16. CRARAE, Inveraray ♿ (only Lower Gardens)

(The National Trust for Scotland)

A spectacular 50 acre garden in a dramatic setting. Crarae has a wonderful collection of woody plants centered on the Crarae Burn, which is spanned by several bridges and tumbles through a rocky gorge in a series of cascades. A wide variety of shrubs and trees, chosen for spring flowering and autumn colour grow in the shelter of towering conifers and the lush, naturalistic planting and rushing water gives the garden the feel of a valley in the Himalayas. Sturdy shoes advised. 11 miles south of Inveraray / 14 miles north of Lochgilphead on A83.

Dogs permitted on a short lead only.

Admission £5.00 Concessions £4.00 Under 5s free Family £14.00 (Correct at time of going to press)

SATURDAY & SUNDAY 11 & 12 JUNE 9.30am - 6pm

Donation to Scotland's Gardens Scheme

---

17 . CRINAN HOTEL GARDEN, Crinan

(Mr & Mrs N Ryan)

Small rock garden with azaleas and rhododendrons created into a steep hillside over a century ago with steps leading to a sheltered, secluded garden with sloping lawns, herbaceous beds and spectacular views of the canal and Crinan Loch. Lochgilphead A83, then A816 to Oban, then A841 Cairnbaan to Crinan. Raffle of a painting of flowers by Frances Macdonald. Teas in coffee shop.

Admission £2.00 Accompanied children free

SATURDAY 7 MAY Noon - 5pm

40% to Feedback Madagascar   60% net to SGS Charities

---

18. DRUIMAVUIC HOUSE, Appin

(Mr & Mrs Newman Burberry)

Stream, wall and woodland gardens with lovely views over Loch Creran. Spring bulbs, rhododendrons, azaleas, primulas, meconopsis, violas. Dogs on lead please. Plant stall. Route A828 Oban/Fort William, 4 miles south of Appin. At either end of new bridge bear left at roundabout. At the north end road is signed Invercreran, at the south end road is signed "Local Traffic". Two miles from either end, look for private road where public signs warn of flooding.

Admission £2.00 Children free

DAILY APRIL, MAY & JUNE 10am - 6pm

30% to Alzheimer Scotland - Action on Dementia (Oban & Lorne Branch)   70% net to SGS Charities

---

19. DRUIMNEIL HOUSE, Port Appin

(Mrs J Glaisher)

Gardener - Mr Andrew Ritchie

Ten acre garden overlooking Loch Linnhe with many fine varieties of mature trees and rhododendrons and other woodland shrubs. Home made teas available. Turn in Appin off A828   (Connel/Fort William road). 2 miles, sharp left at Airds Hotel, second house on right. Lunches by prior arrangement. Tel: 01631 730228. Plants for sale. Sorry no dogs.

Admission £1.50 Children free

OPEN DAILY 1 APRIL - 31 OCTOBER 9am - 6pm

All takings to Scotland's Gardens Scheme

---

20. ECKFORD, By Dunoon

(Mr D Younger)

For many years closely connected with the Benmore Botanic Garden, Eckford has a 4 acre woodland garden of immense charm sited on a hillside. The general public will enjoy the massed blooms of rhododendrons and azaleas, and the specialist gardener will notice unusual specimens of trees and shrubs that have been planted over the past 100 years. This is a wild garden, so sturdy shoes are advised. Eckford lies just off the A815 about 6½ miles north of Dunoon and ½ mile south of Benmore Garden. Plants for sale when available.
Admission £2.00

OPEN DAILY FROM 9 APRIL - 6 JUNE 10am - 5pm
40% to John Younger Trust   60% net to SGS Charities

---

21. GLECKNABAE, Rothesay   & (partially)

(Iain & Margaret Gimblett)

A south-facing hillside garden in the least known part of the unexplored island of Bute with magnificent views to the mountains of Arran. Award winning courtyard garden with rock, boulder and bog gardens created around the house. This is a young garden, small, unusual, welcoming and inspirational. Route: B875 to Ettrick Bay, signposted off the coast road between Rhubodach and Rothesay; continue to end of 'made up' road; approximately 5 miles.
Admission £2.50 Children £1.00 to include soup & roll lunch or teas with home baking.

SUNDAY 3 JULY 10.30am - 4.30pm
Also by appointment from Spring to Autumn Tel: 01700 505655
Individuals or small parties welcome
40% to The British Heart Foundation   60% net to SGS Charities

---

22. JURA HOUSE, Ardfin, Isle of Jura

(The Ardfin Trust)

Organic walled garden with wide variety of unusual plants and shrubs, including large Australasian collection. Also interesting woodland and cliff walk, spectacular views. Points of historical interest, abundant wild life and flowers. Plant stall. Tea tent June, July and August. Toilet. 5 miles east from ferry terminal on A846. Ferries to Islay from Kennacraig by Tarbert.
Admission £2.50 Students £1.00 Children up to 16 free

OPEN ALL YEAR 9am - 5pm
Donation to Scotland's Gardens Scheme

---

23. KILDALLOIG, Campbeltown   & (partially)

(Mr & Mrs Joe Turner)

Coastal garden with some interesting and unusual shrubs and herbaceous perennials. Woodland walk. Pond area under construction. Dogs on lead please.
Route: A83 to Campbeltown, then 3 miles south east of town past Davaar Island.
Admission £2.00 Accompanied children free.

OPEN BY APPOINTMENT. Tel: 01586 553192.
40% to Royal National Lifeboat Institution   60% net to Scotland's Gardens Scheme

---

24. KINLOCHLAICH HOUSE GARDENS, Appin   ♿ (Gravel paths sloping)

(Mr & Mrs D E Hutchison & Miss F M M Hutchison)

Walled garden, incorporating the West Highlands' largest Nursery Garden Centre. Garden with beds of alpines, heathers, primulas, shrubs, rhododendrons, azaleas and herbaceous plants. Fruiting and flowering shrubs and trees. Woodland walk. Spring garden. Route: A828. Oban 18 miles, Fort William 27 miles. Bus stops at gate by Police Station.

Admission £2.00

OPEN ALL YEAR 9.30am - 5.30pm or dusk except Sundays October - March

***(Sundays April - September 10.30am - 5.30pm) Closed Christmas & New Year.** Except by appt.*

40% to Appin Village Hall   60% net to SGS Charities

---

25. STRACHUR HOUSE FLOWER & WOODLAND GARDENS ♿

(Sir Charles & Lady Maclean)

Directly behind Strachur House, the flower garden is sheltered by magnificent beeches, limes, ancient yews and Japanese maples. There are herbaceous borders, a burnside rhododendron and azalea walk and a rockery. Old fashioned and species roses, lilies, tulips, spring bulbs and Himalayan poppies make a varied display in this informal haven of beauty and tranquillity. The garden gives onto Strachur Park, laid out by General Campbell in 1782, which offers spectacular walks through natural woodlands with 200-year-old trees, rare shrubs and a lochan rich in native wildlife. Teas. Plant stall. Route: turn off A815 at Strachur House Farm entrance; park in farm square.

Admission £2.50   Children 50p

FLOWER GARDEN OPEN SATURDAYS & SUNDAYS:

30 APRIL & 1MAY,   28 & 29 MAY,   2 & 3 JULY   1 - 5pm

40% to CLASP   60% net to SGS Charities

---

26. TOROSAY CASTLE & GARDENS, Isle of Mull

(Mr Christopher James)

Torosay is a beautiful and welcoming family home completed in 1858 by David Bryce in the Scottish Baronial style and is surrounded by 12 acres of spectacular contrasting gardens which include formal terraces and an impressive Italian statue walk, surrounded by informal woodland and water gardens. Many rare and tender plants. Tearoom. Gift shop. Adventure playground. Free parking. Groups welcome. 1½ miles from Craignure, A849 south. Miniature rail steam/diesel from Craignure. Regular daily ferry service from Oban to Craignure.

Admission to Castle & Gardens £5.50   Children £2.25   Concessions £5.00

Castle open 25 March - 31 October.   10.30am - 5.00pm

GARDENS OPEN ALL YEAR

with reduced admission when Castle closed

Donation to Scotland's Gardens Scheme

✿ 27.   26 KILMARTIN, Lochgilphead   ♿ (partially)

(Mrs M A Rayner)

Mixed borders, roses, perennials, large rock garden, wild garden, snowdrops, bulbs, trees, azaleas and rhododendrons. Steps to burn. Free range hens. Play area. Teas on Mondays and Thursday or by appointment. Plant stall. Route: A82 - 8 miles north of Lochgilphead in village of Kilmartin.

Admission £2.50

OPEN 10.30am - DUSK   1 JUNE - 30 SEPTEMBER

Or   BY APPOINTMENT Tel: 01546 510215

40% between Zambesi Mission and Mid Argyll Link CLub   60% net to SGS Charities

AYRSHIRE

Joint District Organisers: **Mrs R F Cuninghame,** Caprington Castle,
      Kilmarnock KA2 9AA
      Mrs John Greenall, Lagg House, Dunure KA7 4LE

Area Organisers: **Mrs Michael Findlay**, Carnell, Hurlford, Kilmarnock KA1 5JS
      Mrs R Lewis, St. John's Cottage, Maybole KA19 7LN
      Mrs John Mackay, Pierhill, Annbank, Ayr KA6 5AW
      Mrs R McIntyre, Sorn Castle, Mauchline KA5 6HR

Hon. Treasurer: **Mr Hywel Davies,** Peatland, Gatehead, Kilmarnock

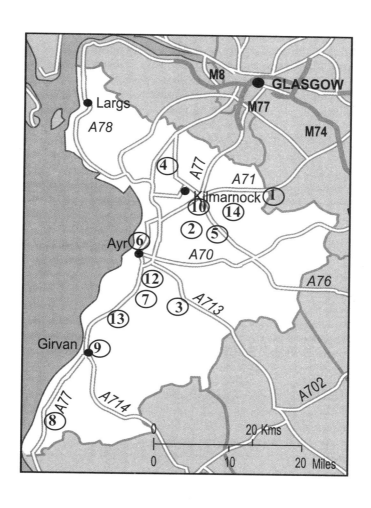

DATES OF OPENING

Glendoune, Girvan	Sunday 1 May	2 - 5pm
Avonhill Cottage, Drumclog	Sunday 15 May	2 - 5pm
Knockdolian, Colmonell	Sunday 22 May	2 - 5pm
Doonholm, Alloway	Saturday 28 May	2 - 5pm
Borlandhills, Dunlop	Sunday 29 May	2 - 5pm
Barnweil, Craigie	Sunday 5 June	2 - 5pm
Ladyburn, By Maybole	Sat & Sun 9 & 10 July	2 - 5pm
Penkill Castle, near Girvan	Sunday 17 July	2 - 5pm
Carnell, Hurlford	Sunday 24 July	2 - 5pm
Skeldon, Dalrymple	Sunday 31 July	2 - 5pm
Blairquhan, Straiton, Maybole	Sunday 7 August	1.30 - 4.15pm
Moorholm, Rowallan	Sunday 14 August	2 - 5pm

1. AVONHILL COTTAGE, Drumclog, Strathaven   (partly)

(Mr & Mrs E Chang)

A maturing garden of approximately 3.5 acres on an exposed site formerly fields and vegetable garden. The planting is varied and includes a woodland shelter belt and herbaceous plants, with 3 ponds and a bank of rhododendrons overlooking the river. Route: 5 miles from Strathaven on the A71 15 miles from Kilmarnock on A71 Drumclog Memorial Kirk turn onto B745 to Muirkirk. Avonhill is on right over hump back bridge. Teas available locally.

Admission £3.00 Children free

SUNDAY 15 MAY 2-5pm

40% to Cats Protection League   60% net to SGS Charities.

2. BARNWEIL, Craigie, near Kilmarnock &

(Mr & Mrs Ronald Alexander)

The garden was started over 30 years ago, and is now nearing maturity, including the beech and holly hedges, planted to give much needed shelter and which are now such a feature of the garden. Formally planned and colour co-ordinated herbaceous and rose borders near the house give way to the woodland garden beyond, which features; rhododendron, azaleas, acers, ferns, hostas, meconopsis and primulas. Recent plantings include the development of the golden borders in the woodland garden and a bed of David Austin roses nearer the house. On a clear day there are fine views to the north for 60 - 70 miles to Ben Lomond and beyond. Home baked teas. Plant Stall. Cars free. Craigie 2 miles. Route: From A77 turn east at Bogend Toll, B730 Tarbolton. 2 miles, on turn right to Barnweil.

Admission £3.00 School children free

SUNDAY 5 JUNE 2 - 5pm

40% to Tarbolton Parish Church   60% net to SGS Charities

3. BLAIRQUHAN, Straiton, Maybole &

(Mr & Mrs Patrick Hunter Blair)

Regency Castle built by William Burn, 1821 - 1842 for Sir David Hunter Blair 3rd Bart. Sixty-foot high saloon with gallery. The kitchen courtyard is formed with stones and sculpture from an earlier castle. All the original furniture for the house is still in it, there is a good collection of pictures and a gallery of paintings by the Scottish colourists. 3 mile private drive along the River Girvan. Walled garden, pinetum and Regency glasshouse. The Castle is surrounded by an extensive park including an arboretum. There is a tree trail and a shop. Admission price includes a tour of the house. Tea in house. Near Kirkmichael, follow AA signs. Entry from B7045 over bridge half mile south of Kirkmichael.

Admission £6.00 Children £3.00 OAPs £4.00 (4.15 last entry to Castle Gardens. Grounds open till 6pm)

SUNDAY 7 AUGUST 1.30 - 4.15pm

40% to Ayrshire Rivers Trust 60% net to SGS Charities

✿ 4. BORLANDHILLS, Dunlop & (partly)

(Professor & Mrs Michael Moss)

This is a young hilltop garden, with magnificent views of Arran, created over the last 8 years. It combines a surprising variety of habitats from a bog garden with gunnera, primula and great clumps of irises to dry sheltered corners with fine displays of bulbs in late spring, rhododendrons, azaleas and meconopsis. Roses and clematis scramble through hedges and over the buildings. There are many unusual Himalayan plants grown mostly from seed. In the heart of the garden are large vegetable plots which provide for the family throughout the year.

Route: From the centre of Dunlop along main Street, turn left at the Church (right is the B706 to Beith) and garden is .7 mile on the left from Church. Teas and Plant Stall.

Admission £3.00 Children Free

SUNDAY 29 MAY 2 - 5pm

40% between NTS, Dunlop Village Hall and Send a Cow   60% net to SGS Charities

---

5. CARNELL, Hurlford &

(Mr & Mrs J R Findlay & Mr & Mrs Michael Findlay)

Alterations in 1843 by William Burn. 16th century Peel Tower. 5 acres of gardens and lanscaped grounds and 100 metre phlox and shrub border. Extensive and spectacular herbaceous borders around Carnell house. Special display by the Scottish Delphinium Society. Plant sale. Silver band. Ice cream and cream teas. Cars free. From A77 (Glasgow / Kilmarnock) take A76 (Mauchline / Dumfries) then right on to the A719 to Ayr for 1½ miles.

Admission £3.00   School children free

SUNDAY 24 JULY 2 - 5pm

40% between Craigie Parish Church & Craigie Village Hall and British Red Cross Society & Scotland's Children's Hospice   60% net to SGS Charities

---

6. DOONHOLM, Ayr   & (limited)

(Mr & Mrs Peter Kennedy)

Informal gardens in attractive setting on the banks of the River Doon. Mature trees, shrubs and marvellous show of rhododendrons and azaleas. Plant stall. Signposted from Burns Cottage, Alloway and from A77.

Admission £3.00 School children Free

SATURDAY 28 MAY 2 – 5pm

40% to Ayrshire Rivers Trust   60% net to SGS Charities

✿ 5. GLENDOUNE, Girvan ♿ (partly)

(Major J C K Young)
The policies round the house contain naturalised daffodils, rhododendrons, azaleas and fine specimen trees. The walled garden is currently in the process of reconstruction with herbaceous borders, bulbs, shrubs, fruit and vegetables. Route: A77 to Girvan - turn off at Shallochpark roundabout (½ mile). (Teas and plant stall).
Admission £3.00 Children under 12 free.
SUNDAY 1 MAY 2 - 5pm
40% to Erskine Hospital 60% net to SGS Charities

---

6. KNOCKDOLIAN, Colmonell ♿ (partly)

(Lord and Lady Richard Wellesley)
A beautiful garden set within a spectacular landscape of river and hills. 1¼ acres of walled garden. Herbaceous borders, greenhouses and a classical peach case. Extensive rhododendrons and azaleas, all planted within the last 10 years mostly around the house and in the policies and along the river. Large plant stall. Remains of fortified house built c1620. Route: 1½ miles from Colmonell, 3½ miles from Ballantrae on junction of B734 and B7044. (No teas)
Admission £3.00 School children free
SUNDAY 22 MAY 2 - 5pm
40% to Ayrshire Rivers Trust 60% net to SGS Charities

---

7. LADYBURN, By Maybole ♿

(Mr and Mrs David Hepburn)
An old garden that has been extensively re-designed and re-planted. Features include a burnside walk, herbaceous and shrub borders and pond with marginal plantings. In 2003 newly created rose beds were introduced to establish the 4 developing collections of old roses. Plant stall. Teas. Route: Off B7023 /B741 Maybole / Crosshill / Dailly road signposted to 'Campsite'.
Admission £3.50 Children 50p *(No dogs please - except guide dogs)*
SATURDAY and SUNDAY 9 & 10 JULY 2 - 5pm
40% between Hope & Homes for children and Mental Health Foundation 60% net to SGS Charities

---

8. MOORHOLM, Rowallan, Kilmarnock ♿

(Mr and Mrs Andrew Moore)
Moorholm sits in 5 acres formerly farmed by the Moore family: well stocked shrub and herbaceous borders together with container plantings attractively surrounding 'The Plant House'. A waterfowl pond is beyond, delightfully landscaped and sheltering ornamental birds, thus NO DOGS PLEASE. Teas. Plant stall. Route: Just north of Kilmarnock, from A(M77) at Meiklewood interchange take B7038 to Kilmarnock shortly after Kilmarnock town sign turn right on to Kilmaurs Road B751. Moorholm is first house on left.
Admission £3.00 Children free
SUNDAY 14 AUGUST 2 - 5pm
40% to Ayrshire Hospice 60% net to SGS Charities

---

9. PENKILL CASTLE, near Girvan   ♿ (limited)

(Mr & Mrs Patrick Dromgoole)

A series of three Victorian gardens, one formal, one landscaped and one originally for vegetables, linked together by a 'wild walk' overlooking a burn leading to the Penwhapple River. Teas. Plant and other stalls, bagpipes and Scottish dancing. Route: 3 miles east of Girvan on Old Dailly to Barr road, B734.

Admission £3.00   School children free

SUNDAY 17 JULY 2 - 5pm

40% to Barr Parish Church   60% net to SGS Charities

---

10. SKELDON, Dalrymple

(Mr S E Brodie Q.C. & Dame Elizabeth Gloster)

One and a half acres of formal garden with herbaceous borders and arched pathways. Large Victorian glasshouse with a substantial collection of plants. Four acres of woodland garden within a unique setting on the banks of the River Doon. Home baked teas. Silver band on the lawn. Plants stall. Route: From Dalrymple take B7034 Dalrymple/Hollybush road.

Admission £3.00   School children free

SUNDAY 31 JULY 2 - 5pm

40% to Princess Royal Trust for Carers   60% net to SGS Charities

---

National Council for the Conservation of Plants and Gardens

There are 6 National Collections in Ayrshire and Arran

NCCPG

1. 3 Groups of Hydrangea
2. Shasta Daisies
3. Oriental Poppies
4. 3 Groups of Rhododendron
5. Elders
6. Trillium

Visit their web site *www.nccpg.com* or call local information 01292 441430

The National Plant Collection Scheme©

BERWICKSHIRE

District Organiser:	**Mrs F Wills**, Anton's Hill, Coldstream TD12 4JD
Area Organisers:	**Mrs C Bailey**, Summerhill, Beauburn, Ayton TD14 5QY
	Miss Anthea Montgomery, Crooks Cottage, Hirsel, Coldstream TD12 4LR
Hon. Treasurer:	**Col S J Furness**, The Garden House, Netherbyres, Eyemouth TD14 5SE

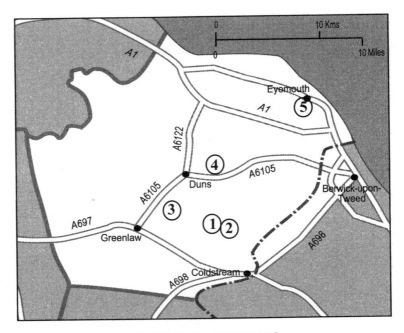

DATES OF OPENING

Bughtrig, Leitholm	15 June–15 September 11am – 5pm, or by appt	
Manderston, Duns	Sundays & Thursdays 8 May –29 September 2 - 5pm	
Netherbyres, Eyemouth	Parties of 10 or more by appointment at any time	
Netherbyres, Eyemouth	Sunday 10 April	2 - 5.30pm
Charterhall, Duns	Sunday 22 May	12 - 5.00pm
Antons Hill, Coldstream	Sunday 3 July	2 - 6pm
Netherbyres, Eyemouth	Saturday 17 July	2 - 5.30pm

1. ANTONS HILL, Leitholm ♿

(Mr & Mrs Wills, Alec West & Pat Watson)

Well treed mature garden which has been improved and added to since 1999. There are wood-land walks including a stumpery and large well planted pond, shrubberies and herbaceous plants together with a restored organic walled garden and greenhouse with a pear and apple orchard. Teas. Large Plant stall. Route: Signed off B6461 west of Leitholm.

Admission £2.50 Children under 16 Free

SUNDAY 3 JULY 2 - 6pm

40% to Oakfield (East Maudit) Ltd 60% net to SGS Charities

2. BUGHTRIG, Near Leitholm, Coldstream   (mainly)

(Major General & The Hon Mrs Charles Ramsay)

A traditional, hedged Scottish family garden, with an interesting combination of herbaceous plants, shrubs, annuals and fruit. It is surrounded by fine specimen trees which provide remarkable shelter. Small picnic area. Parking. Special arrangements, to include house visit, possible for bona fide groups. Accommodation in house possible for 4–8 guests. Half mile east of Leitholm on B6461.

Admission £2.00 Children under 18 £1.00

OPEN DAILY 15 JUNE TO 15 SEPTEMBER 11am - 5pm Contact tel: 01890 840678

Donation to Scotland's Gardens Scheme

---

3. CHARTERHALL, Duns

(Major & Mrs A Trotter)

Mature grounds and walled garden with rhododendrons and azaleas. Also flowered garden of roses and perennial plants situated round a comparatively modern house with small greenhouse and vegetable garden. Teas. Soup and roll lunch. Plant stall. Cake stall. Route: 6 miles south-west of Duns, 3 miles east of Greenlaw, B6460.

Admission £3.00 Children £1.00

SUNDAY 22 MAY 12 - 5.00pm

40% to Friends of Borders General Hospital 60% net to SGS Charities

---

4. MANDERSTON, Duns

(The Lord Palmer)

The swan song of the great classical house. Formal and woodland gardens. Tearoom in grounds. 2 miles east of Duns on A6105. Buses from Galashiels and Berwick. Alight at entrance on A6105.

Admission: £7.00 for house No charge for garden

SUNDAYS & THURSDAYS 12 MAY – 29 SEPTEMBER 11.30am - dusk (House 1.30 - 5pm)

Parties any time by appointment. Tel: 01361 882636 and 01361 883450

Donation to Scotland's Gardens Scheme

---

5. NETHERBYRES, Eyemouth

(Col S J Furness & Perennial (GRBS)

A unique 18th century elliptical walled garden. Daffodils and wild flowers in the spring. Annuals, roses, herbaceous borders, fruit and vegetables in the summer. Produce stall. Teas in house. ¼ mile south of Eyemouth on A1107 to Berwick.

Admission £2.00 Children £1.00

SUNDAY 10 APRIL 2 - 5.30pm

40% to EGunsgreen House Trust

SUNDAY 17 JULY 2 - 5.30pm

Admission to garden £3.00 Children £1.00

Parties of 10 or more by appointment at any time Tel: 018907 50337

40% to Perennial (GRBS) 60% net to SGS Charities

CAITHNESS, SUTHERLAND & ORKNEY

District Organiser: **Mrs Robert Howden,** The Firs, Langwell, Berriedale,
                          Caithness KW7 6HD

Area Organiser: **Mrs Jonny Shaw,** Amat, Ardgay, Sutherland IV24 3BS

Hon. Treasurer: **Mr Colin Farley-Sutton,** Shepherd's Cottage, Watten,
                          Caithness KW1 5YJ

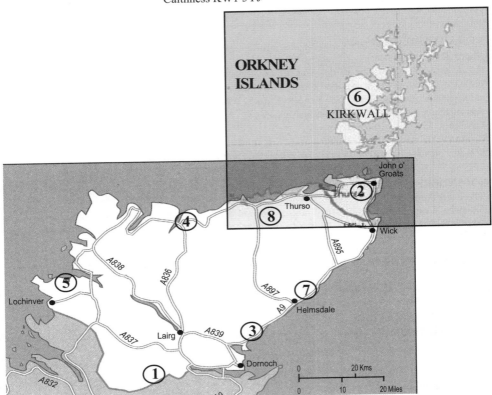

DATES OF OPENING

Kerrachar, Kylesku .... Mid May - mid Sept Tues, Thurs & Suns & By Appt.
Langwell, Berriedale .... By appointment

Amat, Ardgay	Sat & Sun 28 & 29 May	2- 5.00pm
Dunrobin Castle, Golspie	Saturday 25 June	10.30am - 5.00pm
Sandside House, Reay	Sunday 26 June	2 - 5pm
Kierfiold House, Orkney	Sunday 10 July	11am - 5pm
Castle of Mey, Caithness	Wednesday 13 July	11am - 4.30pm
Castle of Mey, Caithness	Thursday 21 July	11am - 4.30pm
House of Tongue, Tongue	Saturday 30 July	2 - 6pm
Langwell, Berriedale	Sunday 7 August	2 - 5pm
Langwell, Berriedale	Sunday 14 August	2 - 5pm
Castle of Mey, Caithness	Saturday 20 August	11am - 4.30pm

1. AMAT, Ardgay   ♿ Partial

(Jonny and Sara Shaw)
For the last twenty years the garden has been mainly forgotten and a new garden is being created using the old one as a guideline. Woodland and a river walk. Take road from Ardgay to Croick.
Admission £3.00 Children 50p
SATURDAY & SUNDAY 28 & 29 MAY 2 - 5.00pm
40% between Croick Church & Help The Aged 60% net to SGS Charities

2. CASTLE OF MEY & GARDEN, Mey, Caithness   ♿

(The Queen Elizabeth Castle of Mey Trust)
Originally a Z plan castle bought by the Queen Mother in 1952 and then restored and improved. The walled garden and the East Garden were also created by the Queen Mother. Teas served in Old Granary. Route on A836 between Thurso and John O'Groats, 1½ miles from Mey.
Admission to Gardens only £3.00 Concession £2.50
Castle and Gardens: £7.00 Concessions £6.00 Children and cars free
WEDNESDAY 13 JULY 10.30am - 4.00pm
THURSDAY 21 JULY 10.30am - 4.00pm
SATURDAY 20 AUGUST 10.30am - 4.00pm
40% Queen's Nursing Institute (Scotland) 60% net to SGS Charities

3. DUNROBIN CASTLE & GARDENS, Golspie

(The Sutherland Trust)
Formal gardens laid out in 1850 by the architect, Barry. Set beneath the fairytale castle of Dunrobin. Tearoom and gift shop in castle. Picnic site and woodland walks. Dunrobin Castle Museum in the gardens. Suitable for disabled by prior arrangement. Stunning falconry display. (Group admission: Adults £5.60, children & OAPs £4.50, family £17.50.)
Castle one mile north of Golspie on A9.
Admission £6.60 Children £4.50 OAPs £5.70
SATURDAY 25 JUNE 10.30am - 5.30pm (Last admission 5pm)
40% to Imperial Cancer Research Fund 60% net to SGS Charities

4. HOUSE OF TONGUE, Tongue, Lairg   ♿ (partially)

(The Countess of Sutherland)
17th century house on Kyle of Tongue. Walled garden, herbaceous borders, old fashioned roses.
Teas. Tongue half a mile. House just off main road approaching causeway.
Admission to garden £2.50 OAPs £2.00 Children 50p
SATURDAY 30 JULY 2 - 6pm
40% to Children First   60% net to SGS Charities

5. KERRACHAR, Kylesku

(Peter & Trisha Kohn)
Plantsman's garden and small nursery begun in 1995, beautifully located in an extremely remote
and wild coastal setting. Wide range of hardy perennials and shrubs. Featured in "The Garden"
and "The English Garden" in 2002. Access only by 25 minute boat journey from Kylesku (£10).
Garden admission £2.50 Children under 12 free Under 16 half price. (boat and garden)
OPEN mid MAY - mid SEPTEMBER Tuesdays, Thursdays and Sundays
All sailings at 13.00 from Kylesku (Old Ferry Pier)
Additional visits for groups by arrangement. Tel: 01571 833288 email:
peter@kerrachar.co.uk
40% to Myfanwy Meredith Melanoma Research Fund   60% net to SGS Charities

6. KIERFIOLD GARDEN, Sandwick, Orkney

(Euan and Fiona Smith)
Victorian country house and walled garden on Orkney's west mainland. Extensive collection of
herbaceous perennials, including meconopsis and primulas. Teas served locally. Route:
B9057 Dounby - Skaill Road. www.kierfiold-house Tel: 01856 841583
Admission £2.00 Children under 12 50p
SUNDAY 10 JULY 11am - 5pm
40% to RNLI 60% net to SGS Charities

7. LANGWELL, Berriedale   ♿

(The Lady Anne Bentinck)
A beautiful old walled-in garden situated in the secluded Langwell strath. Charming access
drive with a chance to see deer. Cars free. Teas served under cover. Plants for sale. Berriedale
2 miles. Route A9.
Admission £3.00 Children under 12 free OAPs £2.50
SUNDAYS 7 & 14 AUGUST 2 - 5pm
Also by appointment. Tel: 01593 751278
40% to RNLI 60% net to SGS Charities

8. SANDSIDE HOUSE GARDENS by Reay, Thurso   ♿ (partially)

(Mr & Mrs Geoffrey Minter)
Old walled gardens restored and well stocked. Sunken rectangular walled garden. Upper
garden with sea views to the Orkneys and Grade A listed 2-seater privy. Terrace with rockery
overlooking sunken garden. Main gate is on A836 half mile west of Reay village. Teas. Plant
stall. There is a splayed entrance with railings and gate lodge.
Admission £3.00 OAPs £2.00 children 50p
SUNDAY 26 JUNE 2 - 5pm
40% to Reay and District Garden Club   60% net to SGS Charities

CLYDESDALE

Joint District Organisers: **Mr Charles Brandon,** Cherry Tree Cottage,
2 Glenburn Avenue, Symington ML12 6LH
Mrs M Maxwell Stuart, Baitlaws, Lamington ML12 6HR

Area Organiser: **Mrs Irene Miller**, West End, 4 Main Street, Carnwath ML11 8JZ
PR - **Mr G Crouch,** 13 High Street, Biggar ML12 6DL

Hon. Treasurer: **Mrs Edna Munro,** High Meadows, Nemphlar, Lanark ML11 9JF

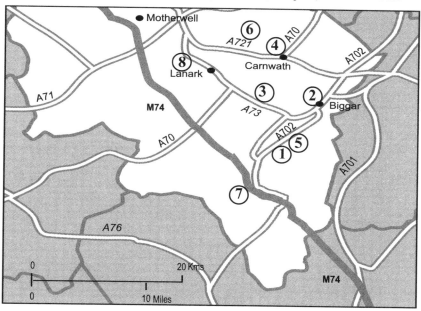

DATES OF OPENING

Baitlaws, Lamington	By appointment June, July, August	
Biggar Park, Biggar	Groups May - July by appointment	
Culter Allers, Coulter	By appointment	
Drakelaw Pottery, Crawfordjohn	By appointment	
Nemphlar Garden Trail, Nemphlar	Sunday 1 May	1.30 - 5.30pm
Biggar Park, Biggar	Saturday 12 June	5.30 - 8.30pm
Dippoolbank Cottage, Carnwath	Sunday 19 June	2 - 6pm
Baitlaws, Lamingoton	Sunday 26 June	2 - 5pm
Carmichael Mill, Hyndford Bridge	Sunday 10 July	2 - 5pm
Biggar Park, Biggar	Sunday 17 July	2 - 5.30pm
Dippoolbank Cottage, Carnwath	Sunday 24 July	2 - 5pm
Carnwath Village Gardens Trail, Carnwath,	Sunday 14 August	1.30 - 6pm

1. BAITLAWS, Lamington, Biggar

(Mr & Mrs M Maxwell Stuart)

The garden is set at over 900ft above sea level and has been developed over the past twenty five years with a particular emphasis on colour combinations of shrubs and herbaceous perennials which flourish at that height. The surrounding hills make an imposing backdrop. Opening in June this year for the first time to enable visitors to fill gaps in their own borders from the large plant stall. Large plant stall. Teas. Route: off A702 above Lamington village. Biggar 5 miles, Abington 5 miles, Lanark 10 miles.

Admission £3.00 Children under 12 Free

SUNDAY 26 JUNE 2 - 5pm

By Appointment JUNE, JULY & AUGUST Tel: 01899 850240

40% to Biggar Museum Trust, Lamington Chapel Restoration Fund 60% net to SGS Charities

---

2. BIGGAR PARK, Biggar   ♿ (partially)

(Mr & Mrs David Barnes)

Ten acre garden, starred in "Good Gardens Guide" and featured on "The Beechgrove Garden". Incorporating traditional walled garden with long stretches of herbaceous borders, shrubberies, fruit, vegetables and greenhouses. Lawns, walks, pools, Japanese garden and other interesting features. Glades of rhododendrons, azaleas and blue poppies in May and June. Good collection of old fashioned and new specie roses in July. Interesting young trees. On A702, quarter mile south of Biggar. Dogs on leads please.

SUNDAY 12 JUNE 5.30 - 8.30 Admission £4.00 to include a glass of wine

Enormous plant sale all home grown

40% to WWF 60% net to SGS Charities

SUNDAY 17 JULY 2 - 5.30pm Admission £3.00 (nice children free)

Tea and biscuits and another Enormous Plant Sale

40% to Cancer Research 60% net to SGS Charities

Groups welcome MAY - JULY by appointment. Tel: 01899 220185.

---

3. CARMICHAEL MILL, Hyndford Bridge, Lanark   ♿ (partially & access to riverbank now possible)

(Chris, Ken & Gemma Fawell)

Riverside gardens which surround the only remaining workable water powered grain mill on the whole of the River Clyde a few miles upstream from the World Heritage site of New Lanark Textile Mill. Machinery working if river levels allow. Informal and wild gardens with fruit and vegetables with herbaceous and shrub plantings with riverside walks. Newly created 2 metre deep still pond. Archaeological remains of horizontal grain mill c1200 and foundry, lint mill and threshing mill activity. Just off A73 Lanark to Biggar road half a mile east of the Hyndford Bridge. Teas served in the mill. Plant stall. Field car parking courtesy Messrs A & A Struthers, Millhill Farm.

Admission to gardens and mill £3.00 OAPs & Children over 12 £2.00

SUNDAY 10 JULY 2 - 5pm

Admission by appointment at any other reasonable time Tel: 01555 665880

40% The Royal Burgh of Lanark Museum 60% net to SGS Charities

---

4. CARNWATH VILLAGE GARDEN TRAIL

Parking at car park at the top of the village on the A70 where the trail plan will be available, the trail through this conservation village commences from the Peebles road down the south side of the main street (A721) calling in at gardens on the way to the Jubilee Garden at St. May's Aisle. Returning by the north side visitors are invited to call in at the Church Hall for home made cream teas, coffee and plant stalls, eventually returning to the car park. Route: A721 from Carluke and west, A70 'Lang Whang' from Edinburgh.

Admission £3.00   Children under 14 free

SUNDAY 14 AUGUST 1.30 - 6pm

40% to Carnwath in Bloom   60% net to SGS Charities

---

5. CULTER ALLERS, Coulter   ⅋ (partially)

(The McCosh Family)

Culter Allers, a late Victorian gothic house, has maintained its traditional one-acre walled kitchen garden which continues to provide vegetables, fruit and flowers for the family. Peas and sweet peas, potatoes and poppies, cabbages and cornflowers, are bordered by box hedges. Areas of the kitchen garden have been opened out into a lawn, a formal rose garden around a well, a herb garden and herbaceous borders. The remainder of the extensive grounds of the house include a woodland walk and an avenue of 125 year old lime trees leading to the Village Church. In the village of Coulter, 3 miles south of Biggar on A702.

Admission by donation

BY APPOINTMENT TEL: 01899 220410

(Looks good in July, August & September)

---

6. DIPPOOLBANK COTTAGE, Carnwath

(Mr Allan Brash)

Artist's intriguing cottage garden. Vegetables grown in small beds. Herbs, fruit, flowers. Garden now extended to include pond, with flowers, trees, etc.   Plant stall. Home made bird boxes and wooden toadstools. Tree house now completed. Teas in the lean to. Route: off B7016, 2½ miles Carnwath. Well signed.

Admission £2.50 Children free

SUNDAYS 19 JUNE & 24 JULY 2 - 6pm

40% to Cancer Relief Macmillan Fund   60% net to SGS Charities

---

7. DRAKELAW POTTERY, Crawfordjohn

(Mark & Liz Steele)

The cottage once formed part of the grounds of Gilkerscleugh House and is now set in woodland and gardens created in the last ten years by a landscape architect and his family. The garden comprises imaginative combinations of perennial, shrub and tree planting surrounding a lawn, terrace, spring fed ponds and Garden Burn. There is an emphasis on bold and vigorous plants that are hardy despite the aspect and elevation of the garden. Teas, water features and a sale of decorative and functional pottery. Sorry no dogs. Route: Located on the road to Crawfordjohn 2½ miles from junction 13 on the M74 and 2 miles from the village.

Admission £3.00 Children Free

BY APPOINTMENT JUNE, JULY & AUGUST Tel: 01864 502748

40% to The British Red Cross 60% net to SGS Charities

---

8. NEMPHLAR VILLAGE GARDEN TRAIL, Nemphlar, Lanark
A varied selection of gardens in spring, with extensive views over the Clyde Valley. A pleasant stroll of 1 mile covers all gardens. Teas in Village Hall. Plant stall. Free parking. Guide dogs only. Route: Leave A73 at Cartland Bridge or A72 (Clyde Valley Road) at Crossford. Admission £3.00   Children under 14 free
SUNDAY 1 MAY 1.30 - 5.30pm
40% to Lanarkshire Cancer Care Trust   60% net to SGS Charities

---

DUMFRIES

District Organiser	**Mrs Sarah Landale**, Dalswinton House, Auldgirth
Area Organisers:	**Mrs Fiona Bell-Irving** Bankside, Kettleholm, Lockerbie.
Hon. Treasurer:	**Mr J. Smith** Kirkmichael Old Manse, Parkgate, Dumfries DG1 3LY

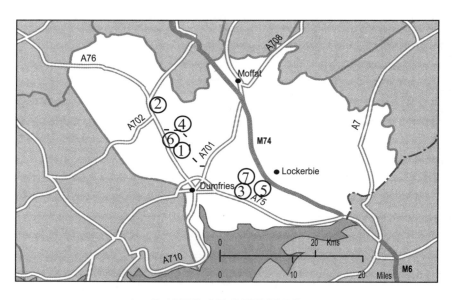

DATES OF OPENING

Dalswinton House, Auldgirth	Sunday 10 April	2 - 5pm
Portrack House, Holywood	Sunday 8 May	12 - 5pm
Dalswinton House, Auldgirth	Sunday 15 May	2 - 5pm
Dabton, Thornhill	Sunday 22 May	2 - 5pm
Dalton Burn, Dalton, Lockerbie	Sunday 5 June	2.30-5pm
Skairfield, Hightae	Sunday 10 July	2 - 5pm
Cowhill Tower, Holywood	Sunday 26 June	2 - 5pm
Hallguards Riverside, Hoddam	Sunday 31 July	2 - 5pm

1. COWHILL TOWER, Holywood

(Captain & Mrs A E Weatherall)

Splendid views from lawn down Nith valley. Interesting walled garden. Topiary animals, birds and figures. Woodland walk. Produce stall. Teas under cover. Holywood 1½ miles off A76, 5 miles north of Dumfries.

Admission £2.50 Children 50p

SUNDAY 26 JUNE 2 - 5pm

40% to Loch Arthur Community, The Camphill Trust   60% net to SGS Charities

2. DABTON, Thornhill

(The Earl and Countess of Dalkeith)

Late 18th century house built of pink stone. Extensive walled garden. Herbaceous border 95 yards long, roses, island beds of trees and shrubs, pond with azaleas and primulas. Woodland walk, vegetable garden, greenhouses. Tea in old stables. Musical entertainment from Scottish Opera. Entrance off A76 between Thornhill and Carronbridge.

Admission £2.50 Concession £2.00

SUNDAY 22 MAY 2 - 5pm

40% to Friends of Scottish Opera (Dumfries & Galloway Branch) 60% net to SGS Charities

✿ 3. DALTON BURN, Dalton, Lockerbie

(Peter and Sue Barbour)

A compact, mature, informal garden extending to 1 acre. Teas and plant stall. Route: From A75 at Carruthers head for Dalton, at Dalton turn left at junction heading for Loachmaben B7020. ¼ of a mile tun left down lane over hump backed bridge, first left.

Admission £2.50 Children 50p

SUNDAY 5 JUNE 2.30 - 5pm

40% net to Sargent Cancer Care   60% net to SGS Charities

4. DALSWINTON HOUSE, Auldgirth

(Mr & Mrs Peter Landale)

In April daffodil walk along woodland and lochside. In May woodland and lochside walks. Cake and plant stall. Home baked teas. Dumfries 7 miles. Dumfries/Auldgirth bus via Kirkton stops at lodge.

Admission £2.50

SUNDAYS 10 APRIL & 15 MAY 2 – 5pm

April opening - 40% to Prov's Pot Leukaemia Research   60% net to SGS Charities
May opening - 40% to Kirkmahoe Parish Church - May   60% net to SGS Charities

5. HALLGUARDS RIVERSIDE, Hoddam   ♿

(Dai and Morag Griffiths)

Riverside (Annan) garden of about 2 acres of former Hoddam Estate Farmhouse, believed to be site of original Hoddam Castle. Yew trees to 800 years of age and wide variety of shrubs and herbaceous species. garden situated beside Hoddam Bridge. Teas.

Admission £2.50 Children 50p

SUNDAY 31 JULY 2 - 5pm

40% to Sargent Cancer Care for Children 60% net to SGS Charities

6. PORTRACK HOUSE, Holywood
(Charles Jencks)
Original 18th century manor house with Victorian addition; octagonal folly-library. Twisted, undulating landforms and terraces designed by Charles Jencks as 'The Garden of Cosmic Speculation'; lakes designed by Maggie Keswick; rhododendrons, large new greenhouse in a geometric Kitchen Garden of the Six Senses; Glengower Hill plantation and view; woodland walks with Nonsense Building (architect: James Stirling); interesting sculpture including that of DNA. Teas. Route: Holywood 1½ miles off A76, five miles north of Dumfries.
Admission £5.00
SUNDAY 8 MAY 12 - 5pm
40% to Maggie's Centre, Western General Hospital, Edinburgh   60% net to SGS Charities

7. SKAIRFIELD, Hightae
(Mrs M F Jardine Paterson)
Immaculate and varied garden surrounding charming 18th century grey stone house. Special feature: perfect walled kitchen garden with rows of fruit and vegetables. Other features include herbaceous borders, greenhouse, shrubs and lawns. Plant stall. Teas. Parking. Route: B7020 from Lochmaben, after approx. 2 miles left to Hightae Village and follow signs. Lockerbie 4 miles.
Admission £2.50 Children under 12 free
SUNDAY 10 JULY 2 - 5pm
40% to Hightae Church 60% net to SGS Charities

DUNBARTONSHIRE WEST

District Organiser:	**Mrs T C Duggan,** Kirkton Cottage, Darleith Road, Cardross G82 5EZ
Area Organisers:	**Mrs J Christie,** Gartlea, Gartocharn G83 9LX
	Mrs James Dykes, Dawn, 42 East Abercromby Street, Helensburgh G84 9JA
	Mrs J S Lang, Ardchapel, Shandon, Helensburgh G84 8NP
	Mrs N P H Macaulay, Denehard, Garelochhead G84 0EL
	Mrs H G Thomson, 47 Campbell St., Helensburgh G84 9QW
	Mrs J Theaker, 19 Blackhill Drive, Helensburgh G84 9AF
Hon. Treasurer:	**Dr D P Braid,** 41 Charlotte Street, Helensburgh G84 7SE

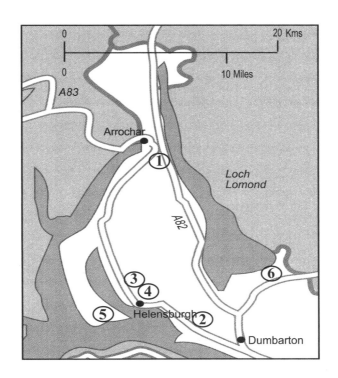

DATES OF OPENING

Auchendarroch, Tarbet .... By appointment

Glenarn, Rhu .... Daily 21 March - 21 September   Sunrise - sunset

Kilarden, Rosneath .... Sunday 24 April   2 - 5.30pm

Glenarn, Rhu .... Sunday 1 May   2 - 5.30pm

Geilston Garden, Cardross .... Sunday 15 May   1 - 5pm.

Ross Priory, Gartocharn .... Sunday 22 May   2 - 5.30pm

Hill House Plant Sale, Helensburgh .... Sunday 4 September   11am - 4pm

1. AUCHENDARROCH, Tarbet

(Mrs Hannah Stirling)

Five acre garden, superbly set on shores of Loch Lomond. Wild garden, woodland walk, wide range of heathers, flowering trees and shrubs including cherries, rhododendrons and azaleas and later, roses and hydrangeas. Regal pelargoniums paticularly notable. Dogs on a lead only.

Route: Immediately south of Tarbet on A82, entrance gate beside Tarbet Pier.

Admission £2.00

BY APPOINTMENT ONLY   TEL: 01301 702240

40% to Friends of Loch Lomond 60% net to SGS Charities

2. GEILSTON GARDEN, Cardross &

(The National Trust for Scotland)
The present design of Geilston Garden was laid out over 200 years ago to enhance Geilston House, which dates back to the late 17th century. The garden has many attractive features including the walled garden wherein a notable specimen of *Sequioadendron giganteum* dominates the lawn and the herbaceous border provides summer colour on a grand scale. In additon a wide range of fruit, vegetables and cut flowers is still cultivated in the kitchen garden. The Geilston Burn winds its way through enchanting woodland walks which provide spring displays of bluebells and azaleas. Tea and shortbread. Plant stall. Sorry, no dogs. Route A814, Cardross 1 mile.
Admission £3.00 Children under 12 free
SUNDAY 15 MAY 1 - 5pm
40% to The Gardens Fund of The National Trust for Scotland   60% net to SGS Charities

3. GLENARN, Rhu, Dunbartonshire

(Michael & Sue Thornley and family)
Sheltered woodland garden overlooking the Gareloch, famous for its collection of rare and tender rhododendrons, together with fine magnolias and other interesting trees and shrubs. Beneath are snowdrops, crocus, daffodils, erythroniums and primulas in abundance. Work still continues in the rock garden (a long project) and there are beehives near the vegetable patch. Collection box, dogs on leads please and cars to be left at gate unless passengers are infirm. On A814, two miles north of Helensburgh.
Minimum donation £3.00 Children and concessions £1.50
DAILY 21 MARCH - 21 SEPTEMBER sunrise - sunset
Special Opening - SUNDAY 1 MAY 2 - 5pm Home made teas, honey and plant stall.
Admission £3.00 Children £1.50
40% to Rhu Parish Church Organ Restoration Fund 60% net to SGS Charities

4. HILL HOUSE, Helensburgh   & (garden only)

(The National Trust for Scotland)
SCOTLAND'S GARDENS SCHEME PLANT SALE is held in the garden of The Hill House, which has fine views over the Clyde estuary and is considered Charles Rennie Mackintosh's domestic masterpiece. The gardens continue to be restored to the patron's planting scheme with many features that reflect Mackintosh's design.
Admission to Plant Sale free. No dogs please. Donations to SGS welcome
 (The Hill House tea room open from 11am.) House open separately 1.30 - 5.30pm.
Admission may be restricted and usual charges apply.
SUNDAY 4 SEPTEMBER 11am - 4pm
40% to The Gardens Fund of the National Trust for Scotland   60% net to SGS Charities

5. KILARDEN, Rosneath, Dumbarton

(Mr & Mrs J E Rowe)
Sheltered, hilly 10 acre woodland with notable collection of species and hybrid rhododendrons collected over a period of 50 years by the late Neil and Joyce Rutherford. Paths may be muddy. Not suitable for wheelchairs. Dogs on leads please. Plant stall. Teas in Church Hall in village. Route: ¼ mile from Rosneath off B833 .
Admission to Garden £1.50   Children free
SUNDAY 24 APRIL 2 - 5.30pm
40% to Friends of St Modan's, Rosneath 60% net to SGS Charities

6. ROSS PRIORY Gartocharn   ♿

(University of Strathclyde)

1812 Gothic addition by James Gillespie Graham to house of 1693 overlooking Loch Lomond. Rhododendrons, azaleas, selected shrubs and trees. Walled garden with glasshouses, pergola, ornamental plantings. Family burial ground. Nature and garden trails. Putting Green. Plant stall. Tea in house. House not open to view. Cars free. Gartocharn 1½ miles off A811. Bus: Balloch to Gartocharn leaves Balloch at 1 pm and 3 pm.

Admission £2.00 Children free

SUNDAY 22 MAY 2 - 5.30pm

40% to CHAS 60% net to SGS Charities

EAST LOTHIAN

District Organiser:	**Mrs Max Ward,** Stobshiel House, Humbie EH36 5PD Tel: 01875 833646
Area Organisers:	**Mrs S Edington,** Meadowside Cottage, Strathearn Road, North Berwick EH39 5BZ **Mrs C Gwyn,** The Walled Garden, Tyninghame, Dunbar EH42 1XW **Mrs W M C Kennedy,** Oak Lodge, Inveresk, Musselburgh EH21 7TE **Mrs N Parker,** Steading Cottage, Stevenson, Haddington EH41 4PU **Mrs J Campbell Reid,** Sylvan Cottage, Goose Green Road, Gullane EH31 2AT
Hon. Treasurer:	**Mr S Edington,** Meadowside Cottage, Strathearn Road, North Berwick EH39 5BZ

DATES OF OPENING

Inwood, Carberry .... Tues, Thurs & Sats 1 Apr- 30 Sept 2 - 5pm
Groups by appt. Tel: (0131) 665 4550
Shepherd House, Inveresk .... Tues & Thurs 2 - 4pm Apr, May & June
& By appointment Tel: 0131 665 2570
Stobshiel House, Humbie .... By appointment Tel: 01875 833646
.... email: wardhersey@aol.com

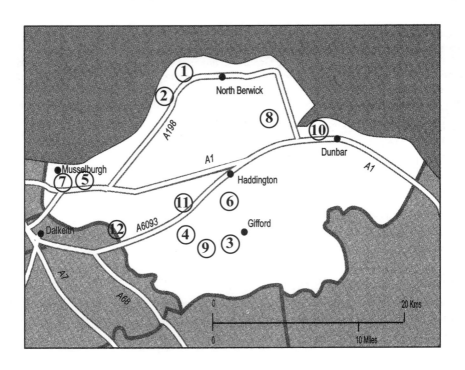

Smeaton Hepburn, East Linton	Sunday 6 March	2 - 4.30pm
Winton House, Pencaitland	Sunday 3 April	12.30 - 4.30pm
Lennoxlove, Haddinton	Sunday 17 April	12noon - 5pm
Aberlady Village,	Sunday 8 May	2 - 5pm
Shepherd House, Inveresk	Sunday 15 May	2 - 5pm
Tyninghame House, Dunbar	Sunday 15 May	1 - 5pm
Humbie House, Humbie	Saturday 21 May	2 - 5pm
Inwood, Carberry	Sunday 29 May	2 - 5.30pm
Gifford Bank with Broadwoodside	Sunday 12 June	2 - 5pm
Tyninghame House, Dunbar	Sunday 26 June	1 -5pm
Gateside House, Gullane	Sunday 17 July	2 - 5pm
SGS Plant Sale, Dalkeith	Saturday 15 October	9.30am - 3.30pm

1. ABERLADY VILLAGE GARDENS   ♿   (mostly)

A collection of diverse gardens within walking distance in the village of Aberlady. Tickets from open gardens. Teas in the Community Hall. Plant Stall.
Admission £3.00 (Includes all gardens) Children free
SUNDAY 8 MAY 2 - 5pm
All to SGS Charities

2. GATESIDE HOUSE, Gullane &

(Mr F Kirwan)
This is a mature one acre garden by the sea, planted for year-round interest with shrubaceous borders, perennial grasses, annual planting, vegetable garden, orchard, fruit cages and large greenhouse. Large number of agapanthus, delphiniums, chrysanthemums and pelargoniums. Route: Plant stall. Follow signs for the beach in Gullane, Hill Road is the second turn on the left. Gateside House is the fourth driveway on the left.
Admission £2.50
SUNDAY 17 JULY 2 - 5pm
40% to Oxfam   60% net to SGS Charities

✿3. GIFFORD BANK with BROADWOODSIDE, Gifford

Gifford Bank &

(Mr & Mrs Mark Hedderwick)
Walled garden filled with herbaceous, shrubs and vegetables. Greenhouses and frames plus two acres of informal garden of mature trees. Plant stall. Route: On B6355 going out of Gifford towards the Golf Course.

Broadwoodside

(Mr & Mrs Robert Dalrymple)
A young garden planted in and around the courtyard of a converted farm steading, rescued from dereliction in 2000. Pond, temple and other follies in the surrounding farmland. Teas in the oak beamed hall. Plant stall. Route: On B6355 going out of Gifford towards the Golf Course.

Admission £3.00 (includes both gardens)   Children under 12 free
SUNDAY 12 JUNE 2 - 5pm
40% to Cancer Research UK   60% net to SGS Charities

---

4. HUMBIE HOUSE, Humbie

(Mr & Mrs Robert Laing)
Large garden with beautiful herbaceous borders, azaleas, rhododendrons, shrubs and vegetables. Lovely walks. Dogs on leads. Teas. Plant stall. Route: off B6368 Humbie Road between A68 and A1.
Admission £2.50 Children under 12 free
SATURDAY 21 MAY 2 - 5pm
40% to East Lothian Macmillan Nurses 60% net to SGS Charities

---

5. INWOOD, Carberry & (with help)

(Mr & Mrs Irvine Morrison)
Approached through an avenue of towering Scots pines and English oaks, Inwood is a place of surprise and delight. Created from scratch over 20 years, the generously proportioned island beds teem with carefully considered combinations of plants and colours that can easily be translated into smaller gardens. Adventurous planting reaches a peak in high summer when shrubs, herbaceous perennials, cascading clematis and billowing roses provide glorious bursts of colour and hints of sweet perfumes. 2 greenhouses with begonia and streptocarpus collections. Pond. Teas and plant stall. No dogs please. Route: 1 mile south of Whitecraig on A6124. Follow signs for Carberry Candles. RHS partnership garden.
Admission £2.00 Accompanied children free
SUNDAY 29 MAY 2 - 5.30pm
All takings to Scotland's Gardens Scheme
Garden open at other times see website: **www.inwoodgarden.com** *Email:* lindsay@inwoodgarden.com

---

6. LENNOXLOVE ESTATE, Haddington

Home of the Duke of Hamilton, set in 460 acres of wooded estate with trees of historical interest and lots to see all seasons throughout the year. Woodland walks along the river Tyne, cherry blossom trees and one 600 year old Sweet Chestnut. Of particular interest is the star-shaped display of snowdrops, resembling the stars on the Hamilton coat of arms. This display surrounds the ash tree, planted by the late Queen Mother.

On the main driveway and the famous tree-lined avenue, Politician's Walk are daffodil displays in abundance, along with Rhododendrons and Azaleas.

Teas, coffees with home-baking and light lunches will be served in the Pavilion Marquee. Various stalls,: including bulbs and plants, fruit and vegetable, local crafts and floral displays.

Admission Gardens and Pavilion Marquee only: Adults £2.50 Children under 14 £2.00

House Tour & Grounds Adults £5.00 Children under 14 £3.00 Guided tours 12 noon and every ½ hour.

For further information: Tel: 01620 823720 Email: *enquiries@lennoxlove.com*

Website: *www.lennoxlove.com*

SUNDAY 17 APRIL 12 noon until 5.00 pm

40% to The Lennoxlove Trust 60% net to SGS Charities

---

7. SHEPHERD HOUSE, Inveresk, near Musselburgh

(Sir Charles & Lady Fraser)

This late 17th century house has been in the same ownership for 47 years. The garden, mostly to the rear, is constantly changing and provides inspiration for Ann Fraser's paintings. The garden has been the subject of numerous magazine articles; ponds, fountains, formal rill, alpine wall, bulb meadow, potager and parterres. Large collection of tulips.

Admission £2.50 Children free

SUNDAYS 17 APRIL & 15 MAY 2 - 5pm

40% to Amisfield Preservation Trust 60% net to SGS Charities

Garden open at other times see website: shepherdhousegarden.co.uk

*Email:*ann@fraser2570.freeserve.co.uk

---

8. SMEATON HEPBURN, East Linton &

(George B R Gray)

Snowdrops at Smeaton, visit the lake walk and enjoy the early spring at Smeaton-Hepburn with snowdrops in abundance, surrounded by majestic trees. Garden centre open. Route: on left going out of East Linton on B1407 to Tyninghame.

Admission £2.00 Children 50p

SUNDAY 6 MARCH 2 – 4.30pm

40% to The Halo Trust (Landmines) 60% net to SGS Charities

---

9. STOBSHIEL HOUSE, Humbie

(Mr & Mrs Maxwell Ward)

A large garden to see for all seasons. Walled garden adjacent to the house, box-edged borders filled with herbaceous plants, bulbs, roses and lavender beds. Rustic summerhouse. Glasshouse. Shrubbery with rhododendrons, azaleas and bulbs. Water garden with meconopsis and primulas. Formal lily pond. Woodland walks. Home made teas. Plant stall. Route: B6368 Haddington/Humbie roadsign, Stobshiel 1 mile.

Admission £3.00 OAPs £2.00 Children under 12 free

BY APPOINTMENT TEL: 01875 833646 Email:*wardhersey@aol.com*

40% to Cancer Research UK. 60% net to SGS Charities

Barbara Findlay 1930 - 2004

Barbara Findlay was the very popular Chairman of SGS from 1991-1996. She brought huge vitality and enthusiasm to this role and devoted a great deal of her time to the Scheme, including visiting gardens, and their owners, all over Scotland.

Together with her husband Neil, Barbara created a wonderful garden at their home Aytounhill, in Fife, where 12 years ago, they built their home, on a site where the previous house had burnt down some years previously, and the garden had become non-existent.

Barbara also took up painting, concentrating on botanical painting, and was becoming a successful artist in her own right. She suffered from poor health on many occasions during the last 20 years, but never complained and was always smiling and cheerful. After her time as Chairman was over, she continued to be involved with SGS in many ways, and was always willing to help if called upon. She is sadly missed by many.

Neil is opening the garden at Aytounhill for SGS this year on the 19th of June.

Aytounhill House, Newburgh
Sunday 19 June 2-5pm

Cluny House, Aberfeldy
1 March – 31 October 10am-6pm

Photographer: Ray Cox

Glecknabae, Rothesay
Sunday 3 July 10.30am-4.30pm
Also by appointment on 01700 505655

Photographer: Ray Cox

Cally Gardens, Gatehouse of Fleet
Sundays 5 June and 14 August 10am-5.30pm
Photographer: Brenda White

Glenarn, Rhu
Daily 21 March-21 September sunrise to sunset
Special opening on Sunday 1 May 2-5pm
Photographer: Brenda White

Stobo Water Garden, Stobo
Friday 27 May 11am-4pm
Photographer: Brenda White

Tyninghame House, Dunbar
Sundays 15 May and 26 June 1-5pm
Photographer: Ray Cox

Kirknewton House, Kirknewton
Sunday 5 June 12-4pm

Photographer: Ray Cox

Scone Palace
25 March-31 October 9.30am-5.30pm (last entry 5pm)

Barshaw Park, Paisley
Sunday 7 August 2-5pm

Baddinsgill, West Linton
Sunday 12 June 2-5pm

Carmichael Mill, Hyndford Bridge
Sunday 10 July 2-5pm
Also by appointment on 01555 665880

Photographer: Val Corbett

Hatton Castle, Turriff
By appointment on Tel: 01888 562279 Fax: 01888 563943
Email: jjdgardens@btinternet.com

Dipoolbank Cottage, Carnwath
Sundays 19 June and 24 July 2-6pm

Photographer: Ray Cox

Arnot Tower, Leslie
Sunday 3 July 2-5pm

10. TYNINGHAME HOUSE, Dunbar ♿

(Tyninghame Gardens Ltd)

Splendid 17th century pink sandstone Scottish baronial house, remodelled in 1829 by William Burn, rises out of a sea of plants. Herbaceous border, formal rose garden, Lady Haddington's secret garden with old fashioned roses, formal walled garden with sculpture and yew hedges. The 'wilderness' spring garden with magnificent rhododendrons, azaleas, flowering trees and bulbs. Grounds include one mile beech avenue to sea, famous 'apple walk', Romanesque ruin of St Baldred's Church, views across parkland to Tyne estuary and Lammermuir Hills. Teas. Dogs on leish please. Tyninghame 1 mile.

Admission £3.00 OAPs £2.00 Children free

SUNDAYS 15 MAY & 26 JUNE 1 - 5pm

40% to Sandpiper Trust - May opening & The Princess Royal Trust for Carers - June opening 60% net to SGS Charities

---

11. WINTON HOUSE, Pencaitland ♿

(Sir Francis Ogilvy Winton Trust)

The Gardens have been substantially improved and extended in recent years extending down to Sir Davids Loch and up into the walled garden. In Spring there is a glorious covering of Daffodils and other colours making way for the cherry and apple blossoms. The café at Winton is well known for its excellent home baking and afternoon teas.

Entrance off B6355 Tranent/Pencaitland Road.

Admission: House tour & grounds: £5.00, OAPs £4.00, children free

Grounds & café only: £2.50,

SUNDAY 3 APRIL 12.30 -4.30pm

40% The Princess Royal Trust for Carers 60% net to SGS Charities

---

12. SGS BRING AND BUY PLANT SALE

undercover at OXENFOORD MAINS, Dalkeith ♿

Excellent selection of garden and house plants, many unusual, from private gardens. All reasonably priced. Sale held under cover. 4 miles south of Dalkeith on A68, turn left for one mile on A6093. Contact telephone number: Mrs Parker 01620 82 4788

Admission free.

SATURDAY 15 OCTOBER 9.30 am- 3.30pm

40% to Cancer Research UK 60% net to SGS Charities

Why not look up the gardens on our website?
www.gardensofscotland.org
PHOTOS AND MAPS

EDINBURGH & WEST LOTHIAN

Joint District Organisers: **Mrs Victoria Reid Thomas,** Riccarton Mains Farmhouse, Currie EH14 4AR

Mrs Charles Welwood, Kirknewton House, Kirknewton, West Lothian EH27 8DA

Hon. Treasurer: **Mrs Charles Welwood**

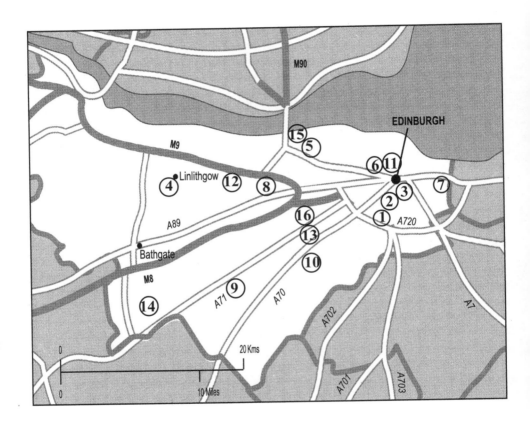

DATES OF OPENING

61 Fountainhall Road, Edinburgh	By appointment	
Newliston, Kirkliston	Wed - Suns inc. 1 May - 4 June	2 - 6pm
Dalmeny Park, South Queensferry	To be announced	
61 Fountainhall Road, Edinburgh	Sunday 3 April	2 - 5pm
Foxhall, Kirkliston	Sunday 17 April	2 - 5pmv
Moray Place & Bank Gardens, Edinburgh	Sunday 8 May	2 - 5pm
South Queensferry Gardens	Sunday 8 May	2 - 5pm
Dean Gardens & Ann Street, Edinburgh	Sunday 15 May	2 - 5pm
61 Fountainhall Road, Edinburgh	Sunday15May	2 - 5pm
Dr Neil's Garden Trust, Duddingston	Sat & Sun 28 & 29 May	2 - 5pm
Suntrap Horticultural Centre, Edinburgh	Sunday 29 May	10.30am - 5pm
Kirknewton House, Kirknewton	Sunday 5 June	12- 4pm
Sawmill, Harburn	Saturday 11 June	11am - 5pm
61 Fountainhall Road, Edinburgh	Sunday 12 June	2 - 5pm
Riccarton Mains Farmhouse, Currie	Sunday 26 June	2 - 5pm
Lymphoy House, Currie	Sunday 17 July	2 - 5pm
9 Braid Farm Road, Edinburgh	Sunday 24 July	2 - 5pm
Annet House, Linlithgow	Sunday 31July	10am - 5pm
61 Fountainhall Road, Edinburgh	Sunday 21August	2 - 5pm
Plant Sale, Kirknewton House, Kirknewton	Saturday 24 Sept	11.30am - 4pm
61 Fountainhall Road, Edinburgh	Sunday 9 October	2 - 5pm

1. 9 BRAID FARM ROAD, Edinburgh
(Mr & Mrs R Paul)

A medium sized town garden of different styles. Cottage garden with pond. Mediterranean courtyard and colourful decked area with mosaic water feature and exotic plants. Plant Stall. Teas. Featured on the BBC's 'Beechgrove Garden'. Near Braid Hills Hotel, on the 11 and 15 bus routes.

Admission £3.00 Children free
SUNDAY 24 JULY 2 - 5pm
40% to Kidney Kids Scotland   60% net to SGS Charities

✿ 2. 36 MORNINGSIDE DRIVE, Edinburgh
(Mrs Elizabeth Casciani)

Private Victorian walled garden (85' x 45'). Owner aims for year-round colour with shrubs, roses and herbaceous planting. Small fruit trees (apple, plum, pear, cherry) and bushes (redcurrent and blackcurrent). Pergola with wisteria, pink jasmine and yellow roses. Tubs of vegetables - potatoes, green bean and courgettes. Teas and plant stall.
Admission £2.50 Children Free
SUNDAY 10 JULY 2 - 5pm
40% between Sightsavers International and WaterAid   60% net to SGS Charities

3. 61 FOUNTAINHALL ROAD, Edinburgh

(Dr J A & Mrs A Hammondl)

Large walled town garden in which trees and shrubs form an architectural backdrop to a wide variety of flowering plants. The growing collection of hellebores and trilliums and the variety of late blooming flowers provide interest from early March to late October. As seen on the 'Beechgrove Garden' and the Chelsea Flower Show programme. 2 small fish ponds have attracted a lively population of frogs. Plant Stall. Teas.

Admission £3.00 Children free

SUNDAYS: 3 APRIL, 15 MAY, 12 JUNE, 21 AUGUST & 9 OCTOBER 2 - 5pm
ALSO by appointment. Tel: (0131) 667 6146
40% to Froglife 60% net to SGS Charities

---

4. ANNET HOUSE GARDEN, 143 High Street, Linlithgow

(The Linlithgow Story)

Restored terraced garden, situated to the rear and an integral part of Linlithgow's Museum has a wide range of flowers, fruit, vegetables and herbs, which were grown in the past to meet the culinary, medicinal and household needs of those who stayed in the house. Also see the unique life -size statue of Mary, Queen of Scots. Route: By road, turn off the M9 Stirling/Edinburgh , from the north - exit 4 from the south - exit 3. From the M8 - junction 4. Follow signs to Linlithgow. Bus & train services operate from Edinburgh & Glasgow. Situated in the High Street, close to the Palace, west of the Cross.

Admission £1.00 Children & conc. 60p (includes entry to the Museum)

SPECIAL SGS OPEN DAY SUNDAY 31 JULY 10am - 5pm
Also open Easter - October inclusive. Mon - Sat 10am -5pm Sun 1 - 4pm (Admission £1)
All takings to SGS Charities

---

5. DALMENY PARK, South Queensferry

(The Earl & Countess of Rosebery)

Acres of snowdrops on Mons Hill. Cars free. Teas will be available in the Courtyard Tearoom, Dalmeny House. Route: South Queensferry, off A90 road to B924. Pedestrians and cars enter by Leuchold Gate and exit by Chapel Gate. Please wear sensible footwear with good grip as paths can be slippy.

Admission £3.00 Children under 14 free

DATE TO BE ANNOUNCED
40% to St Columba's Hospice 60% net to SGS Charities

---

6. DEAN GARDENS & ANN STREET, Edinburgh

DEAN GARDENS (Dean Gardens Committee of Management)

Privately owned town gardens on north bank of the Water of Leith. 13½ acres of spring bulbs, daffodils and shrubs. Entrance at Ann Street or Eton Terrace. Plant Stall. New members welcome to Dean Gardens.

ANN STREET GARDENS

Ann Street is one of the few Georgian streets where the houses on both sides boast their own front gardens. They are particularly pretty in spring and early summer with flowering trees, shrubs and bulbs.

Admission to both gardens £2.00 Children free

SUNDAY 15 MAY 2 - 5pm
40% to the Gardens Fund of the National Trust for Scotland 60% net to SGS Charities

---

7. DR NEIL'S GARDEN, Duddingston Village

(Dr Neil's Garden Trust)

Landscaped garden on the lower slopes of Arthur's Seat using conifers, heathers and alpines. Teas in Kirk Hall. Plant stalls. Car Park on Duddingston Road West.

Admission £2.00 Children Free

SATURDAY & SUNDAY 28 & 29 MAY 2 - 5pm

40% to Dr Neil's Garden Trust   60% net to SGS Charities

---

8. FOXHALL, Kirkliston

(The Gammell Family)

Daffodils and woodland walk. Plant stall. Cake stall. Turn east at lights in centre of Kirkliston, half mile on right, sign at road end, Conifox Nursery. Teas.

Admission £2.00 Children under 14 free OAPs £1.00

SUNDAY 17 APRIL 2 - 5pm

40% to St Columba's Hospice   60% net to SGS Charities

---

9. KIRKNEWTON HOUSE, Kirknewton &

(Mr & Mrs Charles Welwood)

Old landscaped gardens, surrounded by mature trees. Shrubs, rhododendrons spring and herbaceous borders. Wine in old, newly converted, stable building. No dogs please. Route: Either A71 or A70 on to B7031.

Admission £3.00 Children under 14 free

SUNDAY 5 JUNE 12- 4pm

40% to St Columba's Hospice   60% net to SGS Charities

SGS PLANT SALE

KIRKNEWTON HOUSE, Kirknewton   &

Excellent variety of garden plants, shrubs and bulbs. Soup and rolls. Entrance £1.00.

SATURDAY 24 SEPTEMBER 11.30am - 4pm

40% to Childrens Hospice Association Scotland   60% net to SGS Charities

---

10. LYMPHOY HOUSE, Currie   &

(Roy & Doreen Mitchell)

Informal parkland garden with herbaceous borders, shrubbery and speciment trees. Pond and ruin of Lennox Tower. Kitchen garden, stables and woodland walks. Route: A70 to Currie. Turn off into Kirkgate. Right along estate road (opposite graveyard gate). Half a mile on park at bollards. Plant stall. Wine.

Admission £3.00 Children free

SUNDAY 17 JULY 2 - 5pm

40% to Book Aid International   60% net to SGS Charities

---

11. MORAY PLACE & BANK GARDENS, Edinburgh &

(Lord Moray's Feuars)

Moray Place

Private garden of 3½ acres in Georgian New Town, nearing completion of five year major programme of replanting; shrubs, trees, and beds offering atmosphere of tranquillity in the city centre. Entrance: north gate in Moray Place.

Bank Gardens

Nearly six acres of secluded wild gardens with lawns, trees and shrubs with banks of bulbs down to the Water of Leith; stunning vistas across Firth of Forth. Entrance: gate at top of Doune Terrace. Teas.

Admission £2.50 Children free

SUNDAY 8 MAY 2 - 5pm

40% to Marie Curie Cancer Care   60% net to SGS Charities

---

12. NEWLISTON, Kirkliston &

(Mr & Mrs R C Maclachlan)

18th century designed landscape. Rhododendrons and azaleas. The house, which was designed by Robert Adam, is open. Teas. On Sundays tea is in the Edinburgh Cookery School which operates in the William Adam Coach House. Also on Sundays there is a ride-on steam model railway from 2 - 5 pm. Four miles from Forth Road Bridge, entrance off B800.

Admission to House & Garden £2.00 Children & OAPs £1

WEDNESDAYS - SUNDAYS inclusive each week

FROM 1 MAY - 4 JUNE 2 - 6pm

40% to Children's Hospice Association Scotland   60% net to SGS Charities

---

13. RICCARTON MAINS FARMHOUSE, Currie

(Mr & Mrs Michael Reid Thomas)

New 2 acre garden created since 1980 in various stages. Terraces, mixed herbaceoous and shrub borders; varied selection of roses. Teas, weather permitting. Plant stall. Route: A71 from Edinburgh; follow directions for Heriot Watt University; entrance to garden on east side of roundabout. LRT bus no. 45.

Admission £3.00 Accompanied children free

SUNDAY 26 JUNE 2 - 5pm

40% to Oxfam 60% net to SGS Charities

---

14. SAWMILL, Harburn

(Andrew Leslie)

Valley garden built around the ruins of an old water mill. Mixed planting, including herbaceous and bog gardens, with azaleas and asiatic primulas. The garden is open in conjunction with the Harburn Festival (Crafts, Art Exhibition, Dog Show, bouncy castle, etc.) Teas in Community Hall. Dogs on a lead please. Plant stall. Route: A70 Edinburgh/Lanark road, or A71 to West Calder, then B7008.

Admission £2.00 Children under 15 Free

SATURDAY 11 JUNE 11am - 5pm

40% to Harburn Village Hall 60% net to SGS Charities

---

15. SOUTH QUEENSFERRY GARDENS

A selection of small gardens, superb views and a few surprises in the delightful town of South Queensferry. Tickets & maps available *on the day* from ST MARY'S HOUSE, KIRKLISTON ROAD, SOUTH QUEENSFERRY AND THE FORTS, HAWES BRAE, SOUTH QUEENSFERRY. Route: off A90, north of Edinburgh. Teas.
Admission £3.00
SUNDAY 8 MAY 2 - 5pm
20% to Care in the Community   20% to R N L I   60% net to SGS Charities

16. SUNTRAP EDINBURGH HORTICULTURAL & GARDENING CENTRE,
Gogarbank, Edinburgh &

(Oatridge Agricultural College, organised by Friends of Suntrap)
A horticultural out-centre of Oatridge College. Compact garden of 1.7 hectares (3 acres), range of areas including rock and water features, sunken garden, raised beds, vegetable zone, woodland plantings & greenhouses. New home of the Scottish Bonsai Collection. Facilities for professional and amateur instruction, meeting and classroom facilities, horticultural advice and visitor interest. Signposted 0.5m west of Gogar roundabout, off A8 and 0.25m west of Calder Junction (City bypass) off A71. Bus route: Lothian Transit 37. Open daily throughout the year until dusk. Plant sales Monday - Friday 9am -4.30pm. Friends of Suntrap Edinburgh programme of events - *www.ntscentres.org.uk/suntrap*. Advice/booking Tel: 0131 339 7283.
Family day out with plant sales, horticultural advice surgery, homebake teas, stalls and entertainment. Parking for disabled drivers inside main gate other parking opposite.
Admission £2.00 Children & OAPs £1.00
SUNDAY 29 MAY 10.30am - 5pm
20% to Perennial (GRBS) 20% to Friends of Suntrap   60% net to SGS Charities

ETTRICK & LAUDERDALE

District Organiser:	**Mrs M Kostoris,** Wester Housebyres, Melrose TD6 9BW
Area Organiser:	**Mrs D Muir**, Torquhan House, Stow TD1 2RX
Hon Treasurer:	**Mr Miller,** 18 Craigpark Gardens, Galashiels TD1 3HZ

DATES OF OPENING

Bemersyde, Melrose .... Sunday 17 April   2 - 5pm
Crosslee Old Farmhouse, Ettrick Valley .... Sunday 17 July   2 - 5pm
Carolside, Earlston .... Saturday 23 July   2 - 6pm

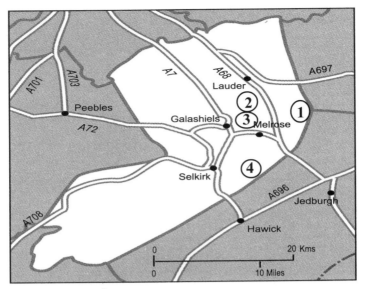

1. BEMERSYDE, Melrose ♿

(The Earl Haig)

16th century peel tower reconstructed in the 17th century with added mansion house. Garden laid out by Field Marshal Earl Haig. Views of Eildon Hills. Woodland garden and river walks. Admission to garden only. Route: B6356. St Boswells via Clintmains or Melrose via Leaderfoot Bridge.

Admission £3.00 Children under 10 free

SUNDAY 17 APRIL 2 - 5pm

40% to Lady Haig's Poppy Factory   60% net to SGS Charities

---

2. CAROLSIDE, Earlston ♿

(Mr & Mrs Anthony Foyle)

18th century house set in parkland. A very traditional elliptical walled garden with a beautiful collection of old roses and herbaceous border. Herb garden, oval rose garden and mixed borders. Teas. Plant stall. Turn off A68 at sign one mile north of Earlston, six miles south of Lauder.

Admission £3.00 Children free

SATURDAY 23 JULY 2 - 6pm

20% to British Red Cross 20% to RNLI 60% net to SGS Charities

---

✿ 3. CROSSLEE OLD FARMHOUSE, Ettrick Valley ♿

(Mr & Mrs James Lockie)

Smallish organic walled garden at 900ft. Soft fruit, flowers, vegetables and herbs in raised beds. Children's play area. Treasure hunt with prizes. Aboretum. Wood with two streams. Erosion control. Picnic area. Dogs on leads please. Cream teas on south facing terrace. Plant stall. Route: from Edinburgh turn off at Innerleithen (B709). Remaining on B709 cross over at Gordon Arms Inn then turn left at next fork, over bridge, follow signs. From Selkirk turn left onto B7009 for 14 miles (pass through Ettrick Bridge at 7 mile mark) Follow signs for car park.

Admission £2.50 Concessions £1.50 Children Free

SUNDAY 17 JULY 2 - 5pm

40% to Ettrick Church 60% net to SGS Charities

FIFE

District Organiser: **Mrs Catherine Erskine,** Cambo House, Kingsbarns KY16 8QD

Area Organisers: **Mrs Jeni Auchinleck,** 2 Castle Street, Crail KY10 3SQ
Mrs Evelyn Crombie, West Hall, Cupar KY15 4NA
Mrs Sue Eccles, Whinhill, Upper Largo KY8 5QS
Mrs Nora Gardner, Inverie, 36 West End, St Monans
Mrs Helen Gray, Arnot Tower, Leslie, KY6 3JQ
Mrs Gill Hart, Kirklands House, Saline KY12 9TS
Ms Louise Roger, Chesterhill, Boarhills, St Andrews KY16 8PP
Lady Spencer Nairn, Barham, Bow of Fife KY15 5RG
Mrs Marilyn Whitehead, Greenside, Leven KY8 5NU
Plant Sale - **Mrs A Cran,** Karbet, Freuchie KY15 7EY
Plant Sale - **Mrs D Skinner,** Lathrisk House, Freuchie KY15 7HX

Hon. Treasurer: **Mrs Fay Smith,** 37 Ninian Fields, Pittenweem, Anstruther KY10 2QU

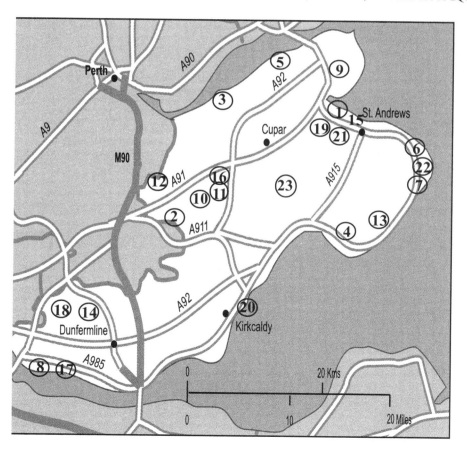

DATES OF OPENING

Cambo House, Kingsbarns	Open all year	10am - dusk
Strathtyrum, St Andrews	Weekdays 1st week of May, June, July,	
....	August & September	2 - 4pm

Cambo Snowdrops, Kingsbarns	Wednesday 23 February	10am - dusk
Wemyss Castle, Wemyss	Sunday 10 April	2 - 5.30pm
Cambo Plant Fair, Kingsbarns	Sunday 17 April	1 - 5pm
Parleyhill & Culross Manse	Sunday 8 May	1- 5pm
Birkhill, near Gauldry	Friday 20 May	5.30 -8.30pm
Kirklands, Saline	Sunday 22 May	2 - 5pm
Gorno Grove House, by Strathmiglo	Sunday 29 May	2 - 5.30pm
Freuchie Plant Sale	Sunday 12 June	Noon - 4pm
Aytounhill House, Newburgh	Sunday 19 June	2 - 5pm
Culross Village Gardens	Sunday 19 June	12.30 - 5.30pm
Kellie Castle, Pittenweem	Friday 24 June	5.30 - 8.30pm
Earlshall Castle, Leuchars	Sunday 26 June	2 - 5pm
Myres Castle, by Auchtermuchty	Friday 1 July	5.30 - 8.30pm
Arnot Tower & Greenhead of Arnot.	Sunday 3 July	2 - 5pm
Wormistoune, Crail	Sunday 10 July	2 - 5.30pm
Crail Small Gardens	Sat & Sun 23 & 24 July	1 - 5.30pm
Earlshall Castle, Leuchars	Sunday 31 July	2 - 5pm
West Kincaple House, by St Andrews	Sunday 7 August	1 - 5pm
Ladies Lake, St Andrews	Sunday 7August	2 - 5pm
Saline Village Gardens	Sunday 14 August	2 - 6pm
Falkland Palace, Falkland	Sunday 21 August	1.30 - 5pm
Balcarres, Colinsburgh	Sunday 28 August	2 - 5.30pm
3 Small Gardens - St Andrews	Sunday 11 September	11am -5pm
Cambo House, Kingsbarns	Sunday 18 September	2 - 5pm
SGS Plant Sale, Hill of Tarvit	Saturday 1 October	10.30am - 4pm
SGS Plant Sale, Hill of Tarvit	Sunday 2 October	11am - 4pm

✿**1. 3 SMALL GARDENS**　　- St Andrews　　　　& 　(2 of 3)
Designed by Derwent Dawes and Betsy Vulliamy
3a The Scores　　　　8 Kinnessburn Road　18 Queens Terrace
(Dr Judith Steel　　　Mrs Moira Weir　　　Mrs Jill Hardie)
Three small, very different, gardens: The first by the sea with a nautical design, the second a
gravel garden with a willow pattern style and the third on a slope with ponds and terraces. All
recently designed and made by the same young couple. It is possible to walk between the
gardens, the total distance is approx. 1 mile. Teas. Route: Go along North Street almost to the
Cathedral, turn left down North Castle Street, left again along the Scores, 2 buildings along from
the castle, second entrance to stone built house on side by the sea.
Admission £3.00　　Children free
SUNDAY 11 SEPTEMBER 11am - 5pm
40% to The Madeleine Steel Memorial Fund for Children with Heart Disease　60% ne t to SGS
Charities

2. ARNOT TOWER & GREENHEAD OF ARNOT

Arnot Tower

(Benjamin & Helen Gray)

New garden created around the ruins of a 15th century tower. Herbaceous borders, terraces, tree rhododendrons. Long pool with fountains, views over Loch Leven.

Greenhead of Arnot

(Mr & Mrs M Strang Steel)

Newly created open garden surrounding renovated farmhouse with newly planted orchard and herbs and vegetables.

Teas   Plant Stall Route: A911 between Auchmuir Bridge and Scotlandwell

Admission £3.50 for both gardens   Children Free

SUNDAY 3 JULY 2 - 5pm

40% to CHAS 60% net to SGS Charities

---

3. AYTOUNHILL HOUSE, Newburgh

(Mr Neil Findlay)

Several mixed borders with a wide variety of shrubs and herbaceous plants. Traditional vegetable garden. Splendid situation. Walk round loch and varieties of trees. Tea and biscuits. No dogs please. Plant stall. Route off A913 7 miles from Cupar and Newburgh.

Admission Adults £3.50   Accompanied Children free

SUNDAY 19 JUNE 2 - 5pm

20% to Dunbog Village Hall 20% to Abdie Church   60% net to SGS Charities

---

4. BALCARRES, Colinsburgh

(The Earl and Countess of Crawford and Balcarres)

19th Century formal and woodland garden; wide variety of plants. Teas. Plant stall. ½ mile north of Colinsburgh off A942.

Admission £3.50 Accompanied children free

SUNDAY 28 AUGUST 2 - 5.30pm

20% to S.W.R.I. 20% to East Neuk Preservation Trust 60% net to SGS Charities

---

5. BIRKHILL, Near Gauldry

(The Earl & Countess of Dundee)

Spring woodland garden which has been restored and extended with rare magnolias and rhododendrons. Soup and rolls. Plant and cake stalls. Route: Off A914 at Rathillet

Admission £10 - includes wine and canapes.

FRIDAY 20 MAY 5.30 - 8.30pm

40% to Cystic Fibrosis Trust 60% net to SGS Charities

---

6. CAMBO HOUSE, Kingsbarns &

(Peter & Catherine Erskine)

Romantic Victorian walled garden designed around the Cambo burn with willow, waterfall and charming wrought-iron bridges. Ornamental potager, breathtaking snowdrops (mail order in February) massed spring bulbs, lilac walk, naturalistic plantings, woodland garden, old roses, colchicum meadow and glowing autumn borders, All seasons plantsman's paradise. Woodland walks to the sea. Featured in 'Country Life' and 'The Garden'. Dogs on leads please. Route: A917.

Admission £3.50 Children Free

WEDNESDAY 23 FEBRUARY 10am - dusk - Snowdrop opening. Plant sale, soup, rolls and teas.

All proceeds to SGS Charities

SUNDAY 17 APRIL 1 - 5pm - Spring Plant Fair. Teas, Cake & Candy, Treasure Hunt.

40% to Diabetes UK   60% net to SGS Charities

SUNDAY 18 SEPTEMBER 2 - 5pm - September Opening Teas, Plant stall.

OPEN ALL YEAR ROUND 10am - dusk

7. CRAIL: SMALL GARDENS IN THE BURGH

(The Gardeners of Crail)

A number of small gardens in varied styles: cottage, historic, plantsman's, bedding. Plant stall. Approach Crail from either St Andrews or Anstruther, A917. Park in the Marketgate. Tickets and map available from Mrs Auchinleck, 2 Castle Street, Crail and Mr and Mrs Robertson - The Old House, 9 Marketgate. No dogs please.

Admission £3.50 Acccompanied Children free

SATURDAY 23 & 24 SUNDAY JULY 1 - 5.30pm

20% to Crail British Legion Hall Fund 20% to Crail Preservation Society 60% net to SGS Charities

8. CULROSS - HIDDEN GARDENS

An ideal opportunity to visit a dozen of Culross truly, inspirational gardens. Normally hidden from view behind the high, stone walls of this historic village, they include the grand terraced gardens of Abbey House, the beautiful gardens of Parleyhill House with breathtaking views over the river Forth, the recreated, medieval gardens of Culross Palace, a contemporary garden with a recycled theme at the local pottery, a cottage garden, a gravel garden and many more.

Free parking is available at the east and west car parks on the B9037. Combined ticket and map available from the Old Schoolyard Community Garden as featured in the BBC's 'Charlie's Garden Army'. Teas & Coffee will be served. Plant stall. No dogs please.

Admission is £4.00. Accompanied children free.

SUNDAY 19 JUNE   12.30 – 5.30pm.

40% to Old Schoolyard Community Garden Fund   60% net to SGS Charities

9. EARLSHALL CASTLE, Leuchars

(Paul & Josine Veenhuijzen)

Garden designed by Sir Robert Lorimer. Topiary lawn for which Earlshall is renowned, rose terrace, croquet lawn with herbaceous borders, shrub border, box garden and orchard. No dogs please. Teas and plant stall. Route: On Earlshall road ¾ of a mile east of Leuchars Village (off A919).

Admission £3.00 Children free

SUNDAY 26 JUNE 2 - 5pm

40% to The Princess Royal Trust for Carers   60% net to SGS Charities

SUNDAY 31 JULY 2 - 5pm

40% to The Liberating Scots Trust   60% net to SGS Charities

10. FALKLAND PALACE GARDEN, Falkland ♿

(The National Trust for Scotland)

The Royal Palace of Falkland, set in the heart of a medieval village, was the country residence and hunting lodge of eight Stuart monarchs, including Mary, Queen of Scots. The palace gardens were restored by the late Keeper, Major Michael Crichton Stuart, to a design by Percy Cane. Tearooms nearby in village. Free car park. Route: A912.

Admission to Garden £5.00 Family ticket £12.50

For Palace admission prices and concessions please see the NTS advert at back of book

SUNDAY 21 AUGUST 1.30 - 5pm

40% to The Gardens Fund of the National Trust for Scotland 60% net to SGS Charities

11. FREUCHIE PLANT SALE   ♿ (with help)

(Major & Mrs A B Cran)

A wide selection of plants: containers, perennial and shrubs will be on sale at Karbet in the centre of Freuchie on the B936. Snack lunch and teas. Baking Stall.

Admission £1.00 Children free

SUNDAY 12 JUNE Noon - 4pm

40% to SSAFA Forces Help 60% net to SGS Charities

12. GORNO GROVE HOUSE, by Strathmiglo   (if dry)

(Sandy & Dianne Matthew)

7 acre developing woodland garden, swathes of mixed native trees with grass paths and avenues. Good views to Lomond hills. A collection of young rhododendrons, azaleas and other shrubs. There is also a pond with water plants and a burn. Plant stall. Soup and rolls. Route: off A91 1 mile east of Gateside. Dogs on leads please. Tea/Coffee and scones. Jazz Band 2 - 4pm

Admission £3.00 Children free

SUNDAY 29 MAY 2 - 5.30pm

40% to CHAS   60% net to SGS Charities

13. KELLIE CASTLE, Pittenweem ♿

(The National Trust for Scotland)

A delightful model of a late Victorian garden, with box-edged paths, fruit, vegetables and many herbaceous plants and roses of the period.

Wine and Roses - £7.50 includes wine and canapes

FRIDAY 24 JUNE 5.30 - 8.30pm

40% to The National Trust for Scotland 60% net to SGS Charities

14. KIRKLANDS, Saline

(Peter & Gill Hart)

Kirklands has been developed and restored over the last 27 years, although the house dates from 1832. Herbaceous borders, rock garden, bog garden, woodland garden with fern collection and walled garden (gradually being restored). Saline Burn divides the garden from the ancient woodland and woodland walk. Teas and Plant Stall. Route: Junction 4 M90 then B914. Parking in the centre of the village. Dogs on a lead please.

Admission £2.50 Accompanied children Free

SUNDAY 22 MAY 2 - 5pm

40% to Saline Community Woodland Project 60% net to SGS Charities

15. LADIES LAKE, The Scores, St Andrews   ♿ (with help - some steps)

(Mr and Mrs Gordon T Senior)
The garden is small, no more than half an acre. It occupies a saucer-shaped curve on the cliff adjacent to St Andrews Castle. In essence, the garden consists of two terraces, one of which is cantilevered over the sea. About 6,000 bedding plants are crammed into half a dozen beds. Teas provided by the ladies of Hope Park Church. Plant stall.   Fiddle and accordion music by Gordon Howe & Nicol Mclaren. Route: from North Street, turn left into North Castle Street, left in front of castle and house is 150 yards on right.
Admission £2.50 Accompanied children free
SUNDAY 7 AUGUST 2 - 5pm
40% to Hope Park Church, St Andrews 60% net to SGS Charities

16. MYRES CASTLE, Auchtermuchty   ♿ (gravel drive)

(Mr & Mrs Jonathan White)
Formal walled gardens laid out in the style of the Vatican gardens in Rome to reflect the Fairlie family's papal connections.   Plant stall. No dogs. Route: On the B936, off the A91
Admission £7.50 includes glass of wine & canapes
FRIDAY 1 JULY   5.30 - 8.30pm
40% to Falkland Heritage Trust 60% net to SGS Charities

17. PARLEYHILL GARDEN & MANSE GARDEN Culross   ♿

(Mr & Mrs R J McDonald & Revd & Mrs T Moffat)
Overlooking the Forth and the historic village of Culross both these gardens nestle in the shade of Culross Abbey and the adjacent Abbey ruins. Parleyhill Garden has evolved in two parts over the years, the earliest part being from the mid - 60's whilst the latter part was begun in the late 80's. The garden of the Abbey Manse is situated in the old Abbey cloister garden. Both are delightful hidden gardens bordered by stone walls and containing interesting displays of old fashioned herbaceous perennials such as phlox, asters, irises, lavender and lilac. Good plant stall selling a selection of plants from the gardens.   Teas. No dogs please (except guide dogs). Disabled access and parking at the Abbey in addition to free parking in the village.
Admission £3.50 Accompanied children free
SUNDAY 8 MAY 1 - 5pm
40% to Culross and Torryburn Church 60% net to SGS Charities

18. SALINE VILLAGE GARDENS

A number of very different styles and sizes of gardens from large, long established, well wooded to recently developed. Plant Stalls. Teas in Church Hall. Route: Junction 4 M90, then B914. Parking in the centre of the village near the bus turning circle, where tickets and maps will be available.
Admission £3.50 Accompanied children Free No dogs please.
SUNDAY 14 AUGUST 2 - 6pm
20% to Saline Church 20% Saline Environmental Group   60% net to SGS Charities

✿ 19. STRATHTYRUM, St Andrews &

(Mr and Mrs A Cheape)
Gardens surrounding house, including small rose garden and newly restored four acre walled garden. Route: Large iron gates with grey urns on right of A91 - ½ mile before St Andrews on Guardbridge side.
Admission £3.00 (House open - Admission £5.00 Child £2.50)
MONDAY - FRIDAY 2 MAY - 27 MAY 2 -4pm
House open -1st week of May, June, July August & September
40% Maggie's Centre   60% net to SGS Charities

---

20. WEMYSS CASTLE, East Wemyss

(Michael and Charlotte Wemyss)
Woodland garden remarkable for its wonderful display of Erythronium revolutum and spring bulbs. Six acre walled garden in the process of complete restoration, begun in 1994 and still ongoing. There are many herbaceous borders with a large collection of roses and clematis. Teas. No dogs please. Route A955 1 mile south of East Wemyss.
Admission £4.00   Children Free
SUNDAY 10 APRIL 2 - 5.30pm
Also open every Thursday 12.30 - 6pm mid April - end August.
40% to S.M.A.R.T. 60% net to SGS Charities

---

21. WEST KINCAPLE HOUSE, by St Andrews   &

(Sandy and Karen Alston)
Another of Fife's delightful walled gardens, surrounded by mature trees. Interesting variety of named espalier apple and pear trees. Herbaceous and formal plantings with pond. eas and Plant Stall. (House not open) Route: Off A91 1½ miles west of St Andrews between Guardbridge and St Andrews.
Admission £3.00 Children Free
SUNDAY 7 AUGUST 1 - 5pm
40% to Cancer Relief   60% net to SGS Charities

---

22. WORMISTOUNE, Crail

(James & Gemma McCallum of Wormistoune)
17th century formal walled and woodland garden. New Pleasance Garden and mosaic celtic cross. Splendid herbaceous border. Largest listed Grisselinia in Scotland. Teas and plant stall. Route: On A917 Crail - St Andrews. No dogs please.
Admission £3.50 Children free
SUNDAY 10 JULY 2 - 5.30pm
20% to Crail Preservation Society   20% East Fife Emergency Trust   60% net to SGS Charities

---

23. SCOTLAND'S GARDENS SCHEME PLANT SALE
at Hill of Tarvit, by Cupar

(The National Trust for Scotland)
Interesting shrubs, perennials and grasses. Clumps of herbaceous plants at bargain prices. Route: A916.
SATURDAY 1 OCTOBER 10.30 - 4pm
SUNDAY 2 OCTOBER 11am - 4pm
40% to East Fife Members Centre of The National Trust for Scotland 60% net to SGS Charities

---

GLASGOW & DISTRICT

District Organiser: **Mr A Heasman,** 76 Sandhead Terrace, Blantyre G72 0JH

Area Organisers: **Mrs A Barlow,** 5 Auchincruive, Milngavie G62 6EE
Mrs M Collins, Acre valley house, Torrance G64 4DU
Mrs C M T Donaldson, 2 Edgehill Road, Bearsden G61 3AD
Mrs V A Field, Killorn, 8 Baldernock Road, Milngavie G62 8DR
Mrs A Murray, 44 Gordon Road, Netherlee G44 3TW
Mr Alan Simpson, 48 Thomson Drive, Bearsden G61 3NZ
Mrs A C Wardlaw, 92 Drymen Road, Bearsden G61 2SY

Hon. Treasurer: **Mr J Murray,** 44 Gordon Road, Netherlee G44 3TW

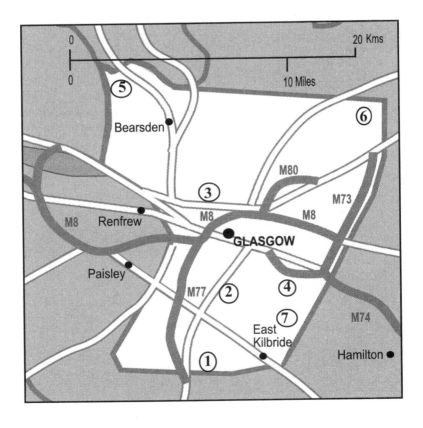

DATES OF OPENING

Invermay, Cambuslang .... April - September by appointment

Kilsyth Gardens . ... Sunday 15 May	2 - 5pm
44 Gordon Road, Netherlee .... Sunday 29 May	2 - 5pm
Killorn, Milngavie.. Sunday 5 June	2 - 6pm
Glasgow Botanic Gardens....................................... Saturday 11 June	11am - 4pm
35 Montgomerie Street, Eaglesham .... Sunday 31 July	2 - 5pm
The Gardens of St Leaonards, East Kilbride .... Sunday 7 August	2 - 5pm

As well as the above garden openings in 2005, the District will have about 7 private garden openings, mainly in Bearsden, if you would like to be invited to any, or all of these please contact the District Organiser or any of the Area Organisers who will pass your request to the garden owners. Addresses of organisers are on the preceeding page.

1. 35 MONTGOMERIE STREET, Eaglesham

(Jean and James Laird)
A colourful country garden featuring beds of annuals and perennials, shrubs and mature trees, pond, many new features and two wells. Home baked teas in nearby Church hall. Plant stall. Route: On B674 through village from East Kilbride to the Ayrshire coast. Guide dogs only please.
Admission: £2.50 Children over 12 £1.00
SUNDAY 31 JULY 2 - 5pm
40% to Macmillan Nurses 60% net to SGS Charities

2. 44 GORDON ROAD, Netherlee

(Anne and Jim Murray)
Mature town garden of approximately one acre containing large trees, rhododendrons and herbaceous borders with many unusual plants. A Japanese garden and water feature are among more recent developments. Plant stall. Refreshments. B767 Clarkston Road past Linn Park gates, turn at Williamwood Drive then second turning on the left. No dogs please.
Admission: £3.00 Children free
SUNDAY 29 MAY 2 - 5pm
40% Erskine Hospital 60% net to SGS Charities

3. GLASGOW BOTANIC GARDENS

(Glasgow City Council)
Glasgow District's Annual Plant Sale will again be held in the spring. A large selection of indoor and outdoor plants and shrubs will be for sale. There will also be an opportunity to view the national Collection of Begonias, the extensive propogation areas and the large collection of orchids. Scotland's largest collection of filmy ferns set in a fairy like grotto will also be open to view and this is particularly appealing to children. Refreshments available. Route: Leave M8 at Junction 17, follow signs for Dumbarton. The Botanic Garden is at the junction of Great Western Road A82 and Queen Margaret Drive.
Any donation of plants beforehand would be welcome: Please contact 0141 942 1295
Admission: Free
SATURDAY 11 JUNE 11am - 4pm
25% to Friends of the Botanics 75% net to SGS Charities

4. INVERMAY, 48 Wellshot Drive, Cambuslang

(Mrs M Robertson)
A plant lovers' garden. Wide variety of unusual bulbs, rock plants, herbaceous plants, shrubs (many named) in a very sheltered, suburban garden. Greenhouse with fuchsias. Something in flower all through the year - a special town garden. Teas. Plant Stall. A730 (East Kilbride) or A749/A724 (Hamilton) from Glasgow. Convenient to M74/M73. Wellshot Drive starts at back of Cambuslang station.
Admission £2.50 Children over 12 £1.00
APRIL - SEPTEMBER Groups by appointment, please telephone first: 0141 641 1632
40% to Children First   60% net to SGS Charities

✿ 5. KILLORN, 8 Baldernock Road, Milngavie

(Vicky and Max Field)
Killorn overlooks the town of Milngavie on a west facing site. Much of the garden has been recently replanted with shrubs and herbaceous perennials, whilst retaining the original late Victorian layout. A new conservatory provides shelter for a variety of tender plants. Refreshments and plant stall. Route: From Glasgow take A81 towards Aberfoyle, on reaching Milngavie, turn right at St Paul's Chruch. Killorn is 150 metres up the hill on right. Please park on South Glassford Street and Baldernock Road but observe parking restrictions. No dogs please.
Admission £3.00 Children over 12 £1.50
SUNDAY 5 JUNE 2 - 6pm
40% to Gael Logan Memorial Trust   60% net to SGS Charities

✿ 6. KILSYTH GARDENS

Aeolia (Mr & Mrs G Murdoch)   **Blackmill** (Mr John Patrick)
Aeolia has a garden of a third of an acre developed since 1960 by the present owners and contains many mature specimen trees and shrubs, a large variety of rhododendrons, primulas, hardy geraniums and herbaceous plants.
Blackmill is on the opposite side of the road from Aeolia and has an acre of ground developed on the site of an old mill. Half of the garden has mature and recent plantings, an ornamental mill lade and pond with the other half consisting of a natural wood and a glen with a cascading waterfall.
Plant stall. Toilets. No dogs please. Route: Take A803 to Kilsyth, turn northwards into Parkburn Road and then follow signs from top of hill.
Admission to both gardens including home made tea £5.00 Children free
SUNDAY 15 MAY 2-5pm
40% to Strathcarron Hospice 60 % net to SGS Charities

---

7. THE GARDENS OF ST LEONARDS East Kilbride

(The Gardeners of St Leonards)
Several prize-winning small gardens that vary in planting style and layout to reflect the owners' interests. Attractions include a fine collection of Bonsai and a collection of cacti and succulents. All gardens are within walking distance of each other. Tickets from Dr T Hussain at 7 Inch Garvie, St Leonards. Light refreshments. Plant stall. Take A749 to Whitemoss roundabout turn onto Calderwood Road. Turn right at the first traffic lights into St Leonards Road and turn onto High Common Road at first roundabout. First left to Calderglen Road then follow signposts. No dogs please.
Admission: £2.50 Children over 12 £1.00
SUNDAY 7 AUGUST 2 - 5pm
40% to Kilbride Hospice Appeal   60% net to SGS Charities

ISLE OF ARRAN

District Organiser: **Mrs S C Gibbs,** Dougarie, Isle of Arran KA27 8EB

Hon. Treasurer: **Mr D Robertson,** Bank of Scotland, Brodick KA27 8AL

DATES OF OPENING

Dougarie. .... Sunday 26 June   2 - 5pm
Brodick Castle & Country Park .... Saturday 16 July   10am - 5pm
Brodick Castle & Country Park .... Saturday 13 August   10am - 5pm

1. BRODICK CASTLE & COUNTRY PARK   ♿ (some)
(The National Trust for Scotland)
Exotic plants and shrubs. Walled garden. Woodland garden. Car park free. Morning coffee,
lunch and tea available in Castle. NTS shop. Brodick 2 miles. Service buses from Brodick Pier
to Castle. Regular sailings from Ardrossan and from Claonaig (Argyll). Information from
Caledonian MacBrayne, Gourock.
Tel: 01475 33755.
Admission to Garden & Country Park £5.00 Concessions £4.00
SATURDAYS 16 JULY & 13 AUGUST 10am - 5pm
40% to The Gardens Fund of the National Trust for Scotland   60% net to SGS Charities

2. DOUGARIE
(Mr & Mrs S C Gibbs)
Terraced garden in castellated folly. Shrubs, herbaceous borders, traditional kitchen garden.
Tea. Produce stall. Blackwaterfoot 5 miles. Regular ferry sailing from Ardrossan and from
Claonaig (Argyll). Information from Caledonian MacBrayne, Gourock. Tel: 01475 337355.
Admission £2.00 Children 50p
SUNDAY 26 JUNE 2 - 5pm
40% to an Island Charity   60% net to SGS Charities

KINCARDINE & DEESIDE

District Organiser: **Mrs E L Hartwell,** Burnigill, Burnside, Fettercairn AB30 1XY

Area Organisers: **The Hon Mrs J K O Arbuthnott,** Kilternan, Arbuthnott, Laurencekirk AB30 1NA
Mrs D White, Lys-na-greyne House, Aboyne AB34 5JD

Hon. Treasurer: **Mr G B McGuire,** Kirkton, St Cyrus, By Montrse DD10 0BW

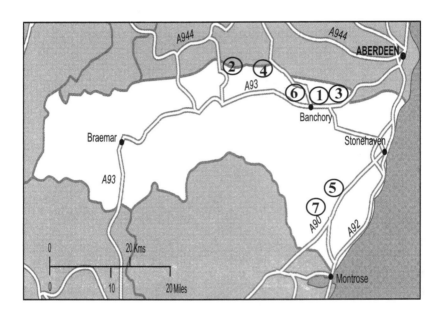

DATES OF OPENING

Inchmarlo House Garden, Banchory	Saturday 4 June	1.30 - 5pm
The Burn House, Glenesk	Sunday 5 June	2 - 5pm
Crathes Castle, Banchory	Sunday 26 June	2 - 5.30pm
Drum Castle, Drumoak	Sunday 3 July	2 - 4.30pm
Findrack, Torphins	Sunday 10 July	2 - 5pm
Douneside House, Tarland	Sunday 24 July	2 - 5pm
Glenbervie House, Drumlithie	Sunday 7 August	2 - 5pm

1. CRATHES CASTLE, Banchory ♿

(The National Trust for Scotland)

This historic castle and its gardens are situated near Banchory, in a delightful part of Royal Deeside. Crathes was formerly the home of Sir James & Lady Burnett, whose lifelong interests found expression in the gardens and in one of the best plant collections in Britain. No less than eight colourful gardens can be found within the walled garden. Exhibitions, shop and licensed restaurant. Sale of plants, garden walks, ranger walks, forest walks. Situated off A93, 3 miles east of Banchory, 15 miles west of Aberdeen.

Admission quoted includes castle, garden, estate and use of all facilities. A timed entry system to the castle applies to all visitors to avoid overcrowding in smaller rooms but there is no restriction on time spent inside. Castle tickets can be obtained on arrival.

Admission (Combined Ticket) £10.00 Child/Concs £7.00 Family £25.00 NTS/NT Members Free
Gardens only £7.00 Car Park £2.00
SUNDAY 26 JUNE 2 - 5.30pm (Last entry to castle 4.45pm)
40% to The Gardens Fund of The National Trust for Scotland 60% net to SGS Charities

---

2. DOUNESIDE HOUSE, Tarland ♿

(The MacRobert Trust)

Ornamental and rose gardens around a large lawn with uninterrupted views to the Deeside Hills and Grampians; large, well-stocked vegetable garden, beech walks, water gardens and new glasshouses. Cars free. Tea in house. Plant stall. Local pipe band. Tarland 1½ miles. Route: B9119 towards Aberdeen.

Admission £2.00 Children & OAPs £1.00
SUNDAY 24 JULY 2 - 5pm
40% to Perennial (GRBS - Netherbyres Appeal) 60% net to SGS Charities

---

3. DRUM CASTLE, Drumoak, by Banchory ♿

(The National Trust for Scotland)

In the walled garden the Trust has established a collection of old-fashioned roses which is at its peak during July. The pleasant parkland contains the 100-acre Old Wood of Drum and offers fine views and walks. Unusual plant sale, children's activities, raffles. Route: 10 miles west of Aberdeen and 8 miles east of Banchory on A93.

Garden & Grounds only £2.50   Children £1.90
SUNDAY 3 JULY 2 - 4.30pm
40% to The Gardens Fund of The National Trust for Scotland 60% net to SGS Charities

---

4. FINDRACK, Torphins ♿ (in parts)

(Mr and Mrs Andrew Salvesen)

Carefully redesigned over the last 12 years the gardens of Findrack are set in beautiful wooded countryside and are a haven of interesting plants and unusual design features. There is a walled garden with circular lawns and deep herbaceous borders, stream garden leading to a widlife pond, vegetable garden and woodland walk. Teas. Plant stall. Leave Torphins on A980 to Lumphanan after ½ mile turn off, signposted Tornaveen. Stone gateway 1 mile up on left.

Admission £2.00 Children 50p
SUNDAY 10 JULY 2 - 5pm
40% to Christ Church, Kincardine O'Neil 60% net to SGS Charities

---

5. GLENBERVIE HOUSE, Drumlithie, Stonehaven

(Mr & Mrs A Macphie)

Nucleus of present day house dates from the 15th century. Additions in 18th and 19th centuries. A traditional Scottish walled garden on a slope with roses, herbaceous and annual borders and fruit and vegetables. One wall is taken up with a fine Victorian conservatory with many varieties of pot plants and climbers on the walls, giving a dazzling display. There is also a woodland garden by a burn with primulas and ferns. Teas. Plant and baking stalls. Drumlithie 1 mile. Garden 1½ miles off A90. NOT SUITABLE FOR WHEELCHAIRS.

Admission £2.50 Children £1 Cars free

SUNDAY 7 AUGUST 2 - 5pm

40% to West Mearns Parish Church   60% net to SGS Charities

---

6. INCHMARLO HOUSE GARDEN, Banchory   ♿ (limited)

(Skene Enterprises (Aberdeen) Ltd)

An ever changing 5 acre woodland garden within Inchmarlo Continuing Care Retirement Community. Originally planted in the early Victorian era, featuring ancient Scots pines, Douglas firs, yews, beeches and a variety of other trees which form a dramatic background to an early summer riot of mature azaleas and rhododendrons producing a splendour of colour and scents. Tea, coffee, homebakes - £3. Route: From Aberdeen via North Deeside Road on A93 1mile west of Banchory, turn right at main gate to Inchmarlo House.

Admission £2.00 Children free

SATURDAY 4 JUNE 1.30 - 5pm

40% to DART (Deeside Aid Romania Trust)   60% net to SGS Charities

---

7. THE BURN HOUSE & THE BURN GARDEN HOUSE, Glenesk ♿

(Lt Col and Mrs G A Middlemiss for The Burn Educational Trust)

The Burn House built in 1791 Grounds of 190 acres including 2½ mile river path by River North Esk and a beautiful walled garden. Tea, stalls and live music in Mansion House. Route: 1 mile north of Edzell. Front gate situated on North side of River North Esk bridge on B966.

Admission £2.00 Children under 12 free

SUNDAY 5 JUNE 2 - 5pm

40% to ANCHOR (Aberdeen Royal Infirmary Cancer Wards) 60% net to SGS Charities

---

LOCHABER, BADENOCH & STRATHSPEY

Joint District Organisers: **Norrie & Anna Maclaren,** Ard-Daraich, Ardgour, Nr Fort Wiliam PH33 7AB

Hon. Treasurer: **Anna Maclaren**

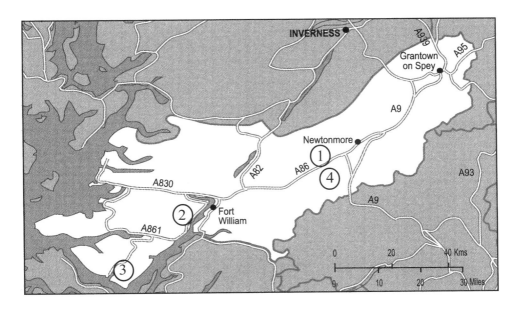

DATES OF OPENING

Ardtornish, Lochaline, Morvern .... Open 1 April - 31 October   10am - 6pm

Ard-Daraich, Ardgour .... Sunday 22 May   2 - 5.30pm
Aberarder, Kinlochlaggan .... Sunday 29 May   2 - 5.30pm
Ardverikie, Kinlochlaggan .... Sunday 29 May   2 - 5.30pm

1. ABERARDER, Kinlochlaggan
(Mr Roddy Feilden & Mr & Mrs Andrew Feilden))
Lovely garden and views over Loch Laggan. Home made teas. On A86 between Newtonmore and Spean Bridge at east end of Loch Laggan.
Combined admission with ARDVERIKIE £3.00. Children under 12 free
SUNDAY 29 MAY 2 - 5.30pm
20% to Marie Curie Cancer Care   20% to Laggan Church   60% net to SGS Charities

2. ARD-DARAICH, Ardgour, by Fort William   &   (in places)
(Norrie & Anna Maclaren)
Seven acre hill garden, in a spectacular setting, with many fine and uncommon rhododendrons, an interesting selection of trees and shrubs and a large collection of camellias, acers and sorbus. Home made teas in house. Cake and plant stall. Route: West from Fort William, across the Corran Ferry, turn left and a mile on the right further west.
Admission £3.00 Children under 12 £1.00
SUNDAY 22 MAY 2 - 5.30pm
40% to Highland Hospice 60% net to SGS Charities

3. ARDTORNISH, by Lochaline, Morvern
(Mrs John Raven)
Garden of interesting mature conifers, rhododendrons, deciduous trees, shrubs and herbaceous set amidst magnificent scenery. Route A884. Lochaline 3 miles
Entrance fee charged
OPEN 1 APRIL - 31 OCTOBER 10am - 6pm
Donation to Scotland's Gardens Scheme

---

4. ARDVERIKIE, Kinlochlaggan ⅋
(Mrs P Laing & Mrs E T Smyth Osbourne)
Lovely setting on Loch Laggan with magnificent trees. Walled garden with large collection of acers, shrubs and herbaceous. Architecturally interesting house (Not open). Site of the filming of the TV series "Monarch of the Glen". On A86 between Newtonmore and Spean Bridge. Entrance at east end of Loch Laggan by gate lodge over bridge. Plant Stall. Home made teas at Aberarder. Combined admission with ABERARDER £3.00 Children 12 free
SUNDAY 29 MAY 2 - 5.30pm
20% to Marie Curie Cancer Care 20% to Laggan Church 60% net to SGS Charities

---

MIDLOTHIAN

District Organisers: **Mrs Richard Barron,** Laureldene, Kevock Road,
                         Lasswade EH18 1HT

Area Organisers: **Lady Borthwick,** Crookston House, Heriot EH38 5YS
                        Mrs A M Gundlach, Fermain, 4 Upper Broomieknowe,
                         Lasswade EH18 1LP
                        Mrs R Hill, 27 Biggar Road, Silverburn EH26 9LJ
                        Mrs E Watson, Newlandburn House, Newlandrig, Gorebridge
                         EH23 4NS

Hon. Treasurer: **Mr A M Gundlach,** Fermain, 4 Upper Broomieknowe,
                         Lasswade EH18 1LP

DATES OF OPENING

Newhall, Carlops	By appointment 01968 660206	
Oxenfoord Castle, Pathhead	Sunday 24 April	2 - 5.30pm
Cakemuir Castle, Tynehead	Monday 30 May	10am -2pm
Newhall, Carlops	Sunday 15 May	11am - 4pm
Penicuik House, Penicuik	Sunday 5 June	2 - 5.30pm
The Old Sun Inn,		
& Riga Studio Cottage, Newbattle	Saturday 11 June	2 - 5pm
Lasswade: 16 Kevock Road	Sat & Sun 18 & 19 June	2 - 5pm
Barondale House,		
Riga Studio & The Old Sun Inn, Newbattle	Saturday 9 July	2 - 5pm
Barondale House Newbattle	Sunday 10 July	2 - 5pm
Plant Sale, Oxenfoord Mains, Dalkeith	Saturday 15 Oct	9.30 am- 3.30pm

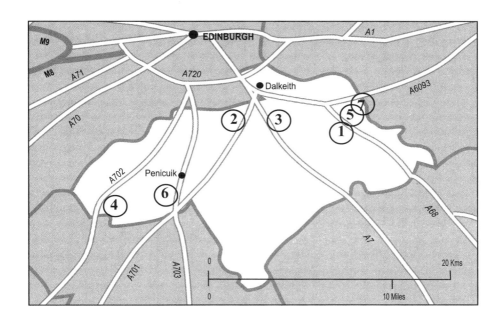

1 CAKEMUIR CASTLE, near Tynehead

(Mr & Mrs Robbie Douglas Miller)

Two acre garden in process of renovation. Narrow access road, parking in field. Coffee/teas in stable yard. Route: Turn off A68 or A7 onto B6457 (Signposted Tynehead) then follow yellow signs.

Admission £2.00 Children £1.00

MONDAY 30 MAY 10am - 2pm

40% to Cancer Research UK   60% net to SGS Charities

2. LASSWADE: 16 Kevock Road

(David and Stella Rankin)

A hillside garden overlooking the North Esk Valley and the ruins of Mavisbank House, with many mature trees, rhododendrons, azaleas and unusual shrubs. These are underplanted with a wide range of woodland plants and there are ponds with primula, iris and other damp loving plants. Higher up the south facing slope there are terraces with rockeries and troughs. The garden has featured in several television programmes and magazine articles. A large plant stall featuring many specialist plants is a feature of this opening. Teas in Drummond Grange Nursing Home (No. 3 Kevock Road) where cars may be parked. Route: Kevock Road lies to the south of A678 Loanhead / Lasswade Road

Admission £2.50

SATURDAY & SUNDAY 18 & 19 JUNE 2 - 5pm

40% to St Paul's and St George's Project 21   60% net to SGS Charities

3. NEWBATTLE GARDENS

BARONDALE HOUSE (**Organic Garden**) (Alec and Diana Milne)

✿ **RIGA STUDIO GARDEN** (Zigfrid and Paula Sapietis)

THE OLD SUN INN (James and Rosemary Lochhead)
Three contrasting gardens - Barondale House beside the River South Esk is an organic garden where flowers compliment the vegetables and fruit. Riga Studio Garden is a Latvian sculptor's garden created by Zigfird Sapietis in memory of his homeland, being mainly trees and grass, wildlife friendly and containing a few of his sculptures. The Old Sun Inn (1690) is a half acre garden with a collection of species lilies, small ponds and a conservatory.
Teas and Plant Stall The gardens are in Newbattle approx. 1 mile from Eskbank roundabout on the B703 (Newtongrange) road.
RIGA STUDIO COTTAGE & THE OLD SUN INN
SATURDAY 11 JUNE 2 - 5pm - £3.00 Children free

ALL THREE GARDENS ON
SATURDAY 9 JULY 2 - 5pm - £4.00 Children free
20% Henry Doubleday Research Association   20% Hopefield Autistic Unit
60% net to SGS Charities

BARONDALE HOUSE, Newbattle (Organic Garden)
(Alec & Diana Milne)
Half acre organic cottage garden attractively situated by River South Esk, where flowers complement year round fruit and vegetables. Old roses and lilies lead to marigolds which help the potatoes and nasturtiums climb the pea nets; slug-eating frogs hide under the waterlilies in the small pond and tagetes keeps whitefly at bay in the greenhouse. Route: 8 miles south of Edinburgh on B703 Newbattle/Eskbank road.
Admission £3.00
SUNDAY 10 July 2 - 5pm
40% to Henry Doubleday Research Association   60% net to SGS Charities

---

4. NEWHALL, Carlops   ♿ (Walled Garden only)

(John and Tricia Kennedy)
Traditional 18ᵗʰ century walled garden in process of restoration. Lovely glen walks.
PLANT SALE straight from the garden, some not often seen in garden centres : eg Macleaya cordata, Kirengeshoma palmata, Chelone obliqua, Inula racemosa, Telekia speciosa, Cephalaria gigantea, Ranunculus aconitifolius 'Flore Pleno', Veratrum viride AND LOTS MORE!   Soup and rolls, coffee/tea and cake.   Dogs on leads.   On A702 Edinburgh/Biggar, exactly quarter of a mile after Ninemileburn and a mile before Carlops.   Follow signs.
Admission £2.50 Children free
SUNDAY 15 MAY 11am – 4pm
Also open by appointment Tel: 01968 660206
40% William Steel Trust   60% net to SGS Charities

---

5. OXENFOORD CASTLE, near Pathhead   ♿ (partly)

(The Hon & Mrs Michael Dalrymple)

Extensive grounds with masses of daffodils and some early rhododendrons. The castle will be open for teas. Route: A68. Opposite Gorebridge turning ¾ mile north of Pathhead.

Admission £2.50 Children under 12 free

SUNDAY 24 APRIL 2 - 5.30pm

40% to Cranstoun Church   60% net to SGS Charities

---

6. PENICUIK HOUSE, Penicuik   ♿

(Sir Robert & Lady Clerk)

Landscaped grounds with ornamental lakes, rhododendrons and azaleas. Home baked teas in house. Route: On A766 road to Carlops, Penicuik 1 mile.

Admission £2.50 Children Free

SUNDAY 5 JUNE 2 - 5.30pm

40% to Church of St James the Less, Penicuik   60% net to SGS Charities

---

7. SGS BRING AND BUY PLANT SALE

Undercover at OXENFOORD MAINS, Dalkeith   ♿

Excellent selection of garden and house plants, many unusual, from private gardens. All reasonably priced. Sale held under cover. 4 miles south of Dalkeith on A68, turn left for one mile on A6093. Contact telephone number: Mrs Parker 01620 82 4788

Admission free.

SATURDAY 15 OCTOBER 9.30 am- 3.30pm

40% to Cancer Research UK   60% net to SGS Charities

MORAY & NAIRN

District Organiser:	**Mrs J Eckersall,** Knocknagore, Knockando Aberlour on Spey AB38 7SG
Hon. Treasurer:	**Dr R Eckersall,** Knocknagore, Knockando Aberlour on Spey AB38 7SG

DATES OF OPENING

Knocknagore, Knockando .... By appointment

Knocknagore, Knockando	Sunday 24 April	2 - 5pm
Dallas Lodge, Dallas	Sunday 5 June	2 - 5pm
Carestown Steading, Deskford	Sunday 12 June	2 - 5pm
Glen Grant Distillery Garden, Rothes	Sunday 12 June	12 noon - 5pm
Bents Green, 10 Pilmuir Road West, Forres	Sunday 19 June	1.30 - 4.30pm
Gordonstoun, Duffus	Sunday 25 June	2 - 4.30pm
Knocknagore, Knockando	Sunday 24 July	2 - 5.30pm
Bents Green, 10 Pilmuir Road West, Forres	Sunday 7 August	1.30 - 4.30pm

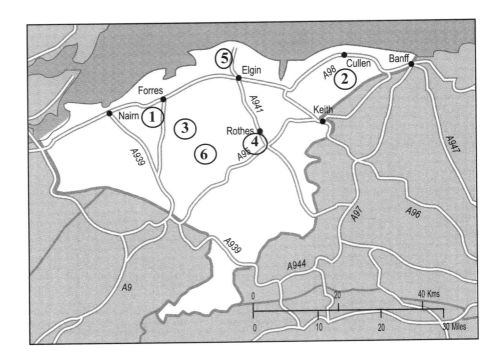

1. BENTS GREEN, 10 PILMUIR ROAD WEST, Forres

(Mrs Lorraine Dingwall)

Small town garden planted in cottage style. Formal pond, unusual plants. Over twenty different clematis, interesting varities of hardy geraniums and hostas. Route: From centre of Forres take Nairn road, turn left at BP garage into Ramflat Road at end turn into Pilmuir Road then sharp left into Pilmuir Road West. Plant stall.

Admission Adults £2.50 Children free

SUNDAY 19 JUNE 1.30-4.30pm

40% to Forres and District Girl Guides 60% net to SGS Charities

SUNDAY 7 AUGUST 1.30-4.30pm

40% to Macmillan Cancer Relief 60% net to SGS Charities

2. CARESTOWN STEADING, Deskford, Buckie

(Rora Paglieri)

The best compliment to Carestown garden was paid by The Garden history Society in Scotland when it described it as "Garden history in the making". In spite of having been started only in 1990 the garden has already received accolades from the press, TV and web (www.CarestownSteading.com). Every year a new addition is made, the latest being the epitome of the modern vegetable plot which is proving to be a great success: 4 year rotation, raised beds, seeping irrigation. Meanwhile trees and shrubs are maturing, the maze is growing, the ducks are reproducing in the three ponds and the atmosphere is as happy as ever. Not to be forgotten is the 'pearl' of the garden, the courtyard with knot beds and topiary now fully mature. Teas on the barbecue area by local Guides. Route: East off B9018 Cullen/Keith (Cullen 3 miles, Keith 9½ miles). Follow SGS signs towards Milton and Carestown.

Admission £2.50   Children 50p

SUNDAY 12 JUNE 2 - 5pm

All takings to Scotland's Gardens Scheme

3. DALLAS LODGE, Dallas, near Forres

(Mr & Mrs David Houldsworth)

Azaleas and rhododendrons, herbaceous and shrub borders in natural woodland setting. Loch garden with islands. Woodland walk. Teas. Plant Stall. Entrance off B9010, six miles from Forres, eight miles from Elgin.

Admission £2.50 Children 50p

SUNDAY 5 JUNE   2 – 5pm

40% to Dallas Village Hall 60% net to Scotland's Gardens Scheme

4. GLEN GRANT DISTILLERY GARDEN, Rothes, near Elgin   ♿ (partly)

(Chivas Brothers)

An award-winning restoration of this delightful Victorian garden created in the glen behind Glen Grant Distillery by Major James Grant, the owner of the distillery. The woodland setting of the enchanting informal garden has been carefully restored to its original Victorian glory. Old woodland walks and log bridges have been rebuilt, the lily pond restored and the lovely mature orchards and rhododendrons have come back into view. The ornamental areas have been replanted with native specimens and plants from America, China and the Himalayas. A visit to the distillery and garden includes exhibitions, audio-visual show about the life of Major Grant and a free dram of Glen Grant pure malt Scotch whisky, which you can also choose to enjoy at Major Grant's Dram Pavilion up in the garden if you wish. Route: On A941 Grantown-on-Spey road at north end of Rothes, about 10 miles south of Elgin.

Admission free, donation to Scotland's Gardens Scheme

SUNDAY 12 JUNE 12 noon - 5pm

40% to Local charity   60% net to SGS Charities

5. GORDONSTOUN, Duffus, near Elgin   ♿

(The Headmaster, Gordonstoun School)

School grounds; Gordonstoun House (Georgian House of 1775/6 incorporating earlier 17th century house built for 1st Marquis of Huntly) and School Chapel - both open. Unique circle of former farm buildings known as the Round Square. Teas. Entrance off B9012 4 miles from Elgin at Duffus village.

Admission £2.00 Children £1.00

SUNDAY 26 JUNE 2 - 4.30pm

All takings to Scotland's Gardens Scheme

6. KNOCKNAGORE, Knockando
(Dr and Mrs Eckersall)
A series of gardens created from rough pasture and moorland since 1995. Comprising trees, herbaceous beds, rockery, courtyard garden and "Sittie Ooterie". Vegetable plot and two ponds, all surrounded by stunning views. Entrance from 'Cottage Road' which connects the B9102 Archiestown to Knockando road with the Knockando to Dallas road.
Admission Adults £2.50 Children 50p
SUNDAY 24 APRIL 2 - 5pm
An opening in April to give the opportunity to see the spring flowers featuring the daffodils, the entry includes tea and biscuits
SUNDAY 24 JULY 2 - 5.30pm - Teas & Plant Stall
Open other times by prior appointment Fax no. 01340 810554
40% to Princess Royal Trust for Carers (Moray Project) 60% net to SGS Charities

PERTH & KINROSS

District Organisers:	**The Hon Mrs Ranald Noel-Paton**, Pitcurran House, Abernethy PH2 9LH
	Mrs D J W Anstice, Broomhill, Abernethy PH2 9LQ
Area Organisers:	**Mrs C Dunphie,** Wester Cloquhat, Bridge of Cally PH10 7JP
	Miss L Heriot Maitland, Keepers Cottage, Hill of Errol PH2 7TQ
	Lady Livesay, Crosshill House, Strathallan, Auchterarder PH3 1LN
	Mrs P Mackenzie, Baledmund House, Pitlochry, PH16 5RA
	Miss Judy Norwell, 20 Pitcullen Terrace, Perth PH2 7EG
	Mrs Athel Price, Bolfracks, Aberfeldy PH15 2EX
	Miss Bumble Ogilvy Wedderburn, Garden Cottage, Lude, Blair Atholl, PH18 5TR
Hon. Treasurer:	**Mr Cosmo Fairbairn** Alleybank, Bridge of Earn, Perth PH2 9EZ

DATES OF OPENING

Ardvorlich, Lochearnhead	1May to 5 June	All day
Bolfracks, Aberfeldy	1 April - 31October	10am - 6pm
Bradystone House, Murthly	May, June & July	by appointment
Braco Castle, Braco	1 February - 31 October	by appointment
Cluniemore, Pitlochry	1 May - 1 Oct and	by appointment
Cluny House, Aberfeldy	1 March - 31 October	10am - 6pm
Glendoick, by Perth	11 April - 10 June Mon - Fri	10 am - 4pm
Monkmyre, Coupar Angus	1 June - 30 September	by appointment
Rossie House, Forgandenny	1 March - 31 October	by appointment
Rossie Priory, Inchture	1 March - 31 September	by appointment
Scone Palace, Perth	25 March - 31 October	9.30 - 5pm
Wester Dalqueich, Carnbo	1 May - 31 August	by appointment

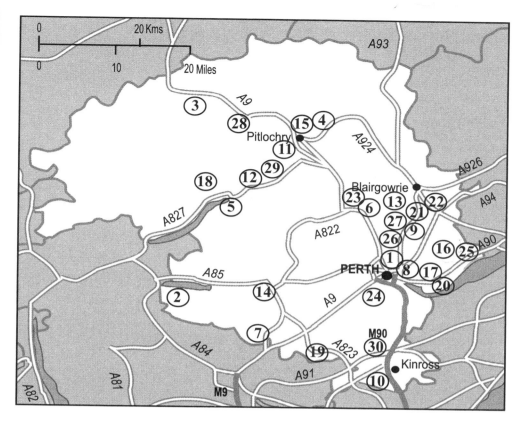

Megginch Castle, Errol .... Sunday 10 April	2 - 5pm
Cleish, Kinross (Cleish Castle & Boreland) .... Sunday 24 April	2 - 5pm
Glendoick, by Perth .... Sunday 1 May	2 - 5pm
Branklyn, Perth .... Sunday 8 May	10am - 5pm
Glendoick, by Perth .... Sunday 15 May	2 - 5pm
Fingask Castle, Rait .... Sunday 22 May	2 - 5.30pm
Delvine, Spittalfield .... Sunday 29 May	2 - 6pm
Meikleour House, by Blairgowrie .... Sunday 5 June	2 - 5pm
Balnakeilly, Pitlochry .... Sunday 12 June	2 - 5.30pm
Explorers, The Scottish Plant Hunters Garden, Pitlochry . Sunday 19 June	11am - 5pm
Murthly Castle, by Dunkeld .... Sunday 19 June	2 - 6pm
Annat Lodge, Perth .... Sunday 26 June	2 - 5pm
Strathgarry House, Killiecrankie .... Sunday 3 July	2 - 6pm
Campsie Hill, Guildtown .... Sunday 10 July	2 - 6pm
Strathtay Gardens, (Pitnacree House & Cloichfoldich) . Sunday 17 July	2 - 6pm
Auchleeks, Trinafour .... Sunday 24 July	2 - 6pm
Glenlyon House, Fortingall .... Sunday 31 July	2 - 5pm
Holestone Lodge, Pool o' Muckhart .... Sunday 31 July	2 - 5pm
Cluniemore, Pitlochry .... Sunday 7 August	2 - 5pm
Drummond Castle Gardens, Muthill .... Sunday 7 August	2 - 6pm
Explorers, The Scottish Plant Hunters Garden, Pitlochry . Sunday 18 September	11am - 5pm
Stobhall, by Perth .... Sunday 23 October	2-5pm

1. ANNAT LODGE, Muirhall Road, Kinnoull, Perth   ♿   (Mostly)

(Mr & Mrs J Kinloch)

One acre town garden created over the last ten years. Mixed planting, lawns, pond, fruit and vegetables. Listed Regency house (not open). Plant stall. Teas. No dogs please. Disabled parking only at house. Route: follow signs to Murray Royal Hospital.

Admission £3.00

SUNDAY 26 JUNE 2 - 5pm

40% to Rachel House 60% net to SGS Charities

---

2. ARDVORLICH, Lochearnhead

(Mr & Mrs Sandy Stewart)

Beautiful glen with rhododendrons (species and many hybrids) grown in wild conditions amid oaks and birches. Quite steep in places. Gum boots advisable when wet. Dogs on lead please. On South Lochearn Road 3miles from Lochearnhead, 4½ miles from St Fillans. Probably no access from Lochearnhead.

Admission £3.00 Children under 12 free

1 May to 5 June ALL DAY

40% to The Gurkha Welfare Trust 60% net to SGS Charities

---

3. AUCHLEEKS, Trinafour

(Mr & Mrs Angus MacDonald)

Auchleeks is a classical Georgian house with a large herbaceous walled garden in a beautiful glen setting, surrounded by hills and mature trees. Teas. Plant stall. Route: North of Blair Atholl turn off A9 at Calvine. B847 towards Kinloch Rannoch, 5 miles on right. Dogs on a lead please

Admission £3.00 Children free

SUNDAY 24 JULY 2 - 6pm

40% to Sandpiper Trust 60% net to SGS Charities

✿ **4. BALNAKEILLY, Pitlochry**   ♿   (If dry)

(Colonel & Mrs Ralph Stewart Wilson)

Mature trees, featuring *Abies procera* (noblis), the 'Noble Fir', originally introduced into Scotland by David Douglas in 1830. These surround a burn and herbaceous borders. Good strolling paths and wonderful views. Dogs on leads please. Route: From Pitlochry take Kirkmichael Road through Moulin, 300 yards on left past Moulin Hotel.

Admission £3.00

SUNDAY 12 JUNE 2 - 5.30pm

40% to The Gurkha Welfare Trust 60% net to SGS Charities

---

5. BOLFRACKS, Aberfeldy

(The Douglas Hutchison Trust)

3 acre north facing garden with wonderful views overlooking the Tay Valley. Burn garden with rhododendrons, azaleas, primulas, meconopsis, etc. in woodland setting. Walled garden with shrubs, herbaceous borders and old fashioned roses. Great selection of bulbs in the spring and good autumn colour with sorbus, gentians and cyclamen. Slippery steps and bridges in wet weather. Not suitable for wheelchairs. Parties welcome. Lunch and teas available by prior arrangement. Please telephone 01887 820344. No dogs please. Limited range of plants for sale. Route: 2 miles west of Aberfeldy on A827. White gates and Lodge on left of road.

Admission £3.00 Children under 16 free

1 APRIL - 31 OCTOBER 10am - 6pm

Donation to Scotland's Gardens Scheme

✿ 6. BRADYSTONE HOUSE, Murthly

(Mr & Mrs James Lumsden)

True cottage courtyard garden converted 9 years ago from derelict farm steading. Ponds, free roaming ducks and hens and many interesting shrubs and ornamental trees. Coffee, tea or lunch by arrangement. Some plants for sale. No dogs please. Route: from south/north follow A9 to Bankfoot, then sign to Murthly. At crossroads in Murthly take private road to Bradystone. Admission £3.00

OPEN BY APPOINTMENT MAY, JUNE & JULY 11am - 4pm Please telephone: 01738 710308

40% to The Salvation Army, Perth   60% net to SGS Charities

✿ 7. BRACO CASTLE, Braco ♿ (Partly)

(Mr & Mrs M. van Ballegooijen)

A 19th century landscaped garden comprising woodland and meadow walks with a fine show of spring flowering bulbs, many mature specimen trees and shrubs, with considerable replanting. The partly walled garden is approached on a rhododendron and tree-lined path and features an ornamental pond, extensive hedging and lawns with shrub and herbaceous borders. The planting is enhanced by spectacular views over the castle park to the Ochils. Please, no dogs. 1½ mile drive from gates at north end of Braco Village, just west of bridge on A822.

Admission £3.00 Children Free

BY APPOINTMENT - 1 FEBRUARY to 31 OCTOBER Please telephone: 01786 880437

40% to The Woodland Trust 60% net to SGS Charities

---

8. BRANKLYN, Perth

(The National Trust for Scotland)

This attractive little garden in Perth was once described as "the finest two acres of private garden in the country". It contains an outstanding collection of plants, particularly rhododendrons, alpine, herbaceous and peat-loving plants, which attract gardeners and botanists from all over the world.   On A85 Perth/Dundee road. Disabled parking at gate.

Admission £5.00 Concessions £4.00 Family £14.00

SUNDAY 8 MAY 10am - 5pm

40% to The Gardens Fund of The National Trust for Scotland 60% net to SGS Charities

---

✿ 9. CAMPSIE HILL, Guildtown

(Brigadier & Mrs Garry Barnett)

An old garden that has gradually been re-designed and replanted within the last 10 years. Features include a rose garden, herbaceous and shrub borders, newly created ponds and woodland walk. Teas and Plant Stall (small). Route: on A93 Perth/Blairgowrie road, north of Guildtown.

Admission £3.00

SUNDAY 10 JULY 2 - 6pm

40% to Guildtown Community Association 60% net to SGS Charities

---

Why not look up the gardens on our website?
www.gardensofscotland.org
PHOTOS AND MAPS

10. CLEISH

⊕ **Cleish Castle** ♿ (partly)

(Judith & Simon Miller)

Originally laid out circa 1620, now only the yew walk remains. The garden has been restored and replanted over the past ten years. Teas in Village Hall. Dogs on leads.

BORELAND ♿

(Neil & Margaret Kilpatrick)

This is now a 10 year old garden featuring woodland trees, shrubs, water and interesting vegetables. Plant Stall. Teas in Village Hall. Dogs on leads.

Route: J5 off M90 take B9097 towards Crook of Devon, Cleish 2 miles follow SGS yellow signs.

Admission £3.00 (includes both gardens) Children Free

SUNDAY 24 APRIL 2 - 5pm

20% to Cleish Village Hall 20% Perennial (GRBS) 60% net to SGS Charities

---

11. CLUNIEMORE, Pitlochry ♿

(Major Sir David & Lady Butter)

Mature garden in a beautiful setting surrounded by hills. Rock and water gardens, lawns, herbaceous and annual border. Roses, shrubs and a short (signed) woodland walk above the garden. Greenhouse. Plant stall. Tea, biscuits and ice cream.

Parties by appointment at any time. On A9 Pitlochry bypass.

Admission £3.00 Children under 16 free

SUNDAY 7 AUGUST 2 - 5pm

Also open by appointment 1 MAY - 1 OCTOBER Please telephone: 01796 472006

40% to The Pushkin Prizes in Scotland 60% net to SGS Charities

---

12. CLUNY HOUSE, Aberfeldy

(Mr J & Mrs W Mattingley)

A wonderful, wild woodland garden overlooking the scenic Strathtay valley. Experience the grandeur of one of Britain's widest trees, the complex leaf variation of the Japanese maple, the beauty of the American trillium, or the diversity of Asiatic primulas. A treasure not to be missed. No dogs please. Route: 3½ miles from Aberfeldy on Weem to Strathtay road.

Admission £3.00 Children under 16 free

1 MARCH - 31 OCTOBER 10am - 6pm

Donation to Scotland's Gardens Scheme

---

13. DELVINE, Spittalfield ♿ (Only near house)

(Mr & Mrs David Gemmell)

The gardens at Delvine are situated on Inchtuthill (the island that floods), an old Roman Legionary fortress abandoned 85AD. In the wild and secluded setting a new arboretum and water project is taking shape below the existing gardens. The area is surrounded by particularly fine and old trees. Teas. Route: on A984 7miles east of Dunkeld, 4 miles sw of Blairgowrie.

Admission £3.00 Children 50p

SUNDAY 29 MAY 2 - 6pm

40% to Back Up 60% net to SGS Charities

---

14. DRUMMOND CASTLE GARDENS, Crieff &

(Grimsthorpe & Drummond Castle Trust Ltd)

The Gardens of Drummond Castle were originally laid out in 1630 by John Drummond, 2nd Earl of Perth. In 1830 the parterre was changed to an Italian style. One of the most interesting features is the multi-faceted sundial designed by John Mylne, Master Mason to Charles I. The formal garden is said to be one of the finest in Europe and is the largest of its type in Scotland. Open daily May to October 2 – 6 pm (last entrance 5 pm). Entrance 2 miles south of Crieff on Muthill road (A822).

Admission £3.00   OAPs £2.00   Children £1.00   Teas, raffle, entertainments & stalls.

SUNDAY 7 AUGUST 1 - 5pm

40% to British Limbless Ex-Servicemen's Association   60% net to SGS Charities

---

15. EXPLORERS, The Scottish Plant Hunters Garden, Pitlochry &

A wonderful new garden overlooking the River Tummel. Planted with a mixture of species and cultivars to represent The Scottish Plant Collectors. Teas at Theatre.   Plant Stall. Route: A9 to Pitlochry town, follow signs to Pitlochry Festival Theatre.

Admission £3.00   Children £1.00

SUNDAYS 19 JUNE & 18 SEPTEMBER 11am - 5pm

40% to Explorers   60% net to SGS Charities

---

16. FINGASK CASTLE, Rait &   (Limited)

(Mr & Mrs Andrew Murray Threipland)

17th century garden with largest collection of topiary in Scotland. Woodland walks, covered bridges, lakes, bamboos etc. Teas.   Route: Half way between Perth and Dundee, (A90)- follow signs to Rait.

Admission £3.00   Children Free

SUNDAY 22 MAY 2 - 5.30pm

20% to Fingask Follies 20% to Refugee Council 60% net to SGS Charities

---

17. GLENDOICK, between Perth & Dundee &   (Only some gardens by house)

(Peter, Patricia, Kenneth & Jane Cox)

Glendoick was recently included in the Independent on Sunday's exclusive survey of Europe's top 50 gardens and boasts a unique collection of plants collected by 3 generations of Coxes from their plant-hunting expeditions to China and the Himalayas. Fine collection of rhododendrons, azaleas, primula, meconopsis, kalmia and sorbus in the enchanting woodland garden with naturalised wild flowers. Extensive peat garden, nursery and hybrid trial garden. No dogs please. Meals and snacks available at Glendoick Garden Centre. Route: follow signs to Glendoick Garden Centre off A90 Perth - Dundee road.

Admission £3.00 School age children free

SUNDAYS 1 & 15 MAY 2 - 5pm & MONDAY - FRIDAY 11 APRIL - 10 JUNE 10am - 4pm

Donation to Scotland's Gardens Scheme and WWF

18. GLENLYON HOUSE, Fortingall   ♿

(Mr and Mrs Iain Wotherspoon)

Interesting garden framed by hedges, with colourful herbacous borders and fruit trees under planted with perennials and annuals. Intensive deep vegetable beds inspired by the late Geoff Hamilton. Teas and Plant Stall. Parking and Art Exhibition at Fortingall Village Hall - 200 yards from garden. Take A827 Aberfeldy, B846 Coshieville turn off for Fortingall and Glen Lyon.

Admission £2.50 Children (over 12 years) 75p

SUNDAY 31 JULY 2 - 5pm

40% to Fortingall Church 60% net to SGS Charities

---

19. HOLESTONE LODGE, Pool o'Muckhart, by Dollar   ♿   (Partly)

(Ronnie Cann & Robert Bradford)

1½ acre garden containing many rare and unusual trees, shrubs and herbaceous plants. There is a small collection of rhododendron species, with peat borders, fernery and various shrub plantings. Several herbaceous borders, some themed by colour and an ornamental grass bed are planted in contemporary style. Water features and rock garden. Some commisioned sculpture. A Japanese courtyard garden, semi-formal potager and terrace displaying tender plants in pots complement the late Georgian House (not open). Water features and a rock garden. No dogs please (except guide dogs). Plant stall. Teas courtesy of the WRI in the village hall. Route: off A91 near 'The Inn at Muckhart'. Park on the main road. *http://www.holestone.net/garden*

Admission £3.00 Children £1.00

SUNDAY 31 JULY 2 - 5pm

40% to THRIVE 60% net to SGS Charities

---

20. MEGGINCH CASTLE , Errol   ♿

(Captain Drummond of Megginch & Baroness Strange)

15th century turreted castle (not open) with Gothic courtyard and pagoda dovecote. 1,000 year old yews and topiary. Astrological garden. Daffodils and rhododendrons. Water garden. On A90 between Perth (9½ miles) and Dundee (12 miles) south side of road. Refreshments.

Admission £3.00 Children free

SUNDAY 10 APRIL 2 - 5pm

40% to All Saints Church, Glencarse 60% net to SGS Charities

---

21. MEIKLEOUR HOUSE, by Blairgowrie

(The Mercer Nairne Family)

Water and woodland garden on the banks of the River Tay. Fine trees, specie rhododendrons and lovely river views. Boat rides. Teas. No dogs please. Quite long grassy walk (300 yards) from car park to garden entrance at Meikleour Lodge. 5 miles south of Blairgowrie of A93 at its junction with the Stanley / Kinclaven Bridge road.

Admission £3.00 Children free

SUNDAY 5 JUNE 2 - 5pm

40% to Rachel House 60% net to SGS Charities

---

30. WESTER DALQUEICH, Carnbo   ♿ (partly)

(Mr & Mrs D S Roulston)

A series of interconnected gardens in three and a half acres by the Ochil Hills, 600 feet above sea level. A wide range of herbaceous and rock plants, shrubs and ongoing development of tree and meadow planting. Guide dogs only please. Tea & coffee available £1. Leave A91 at Carnbo Village Hall, west of Milnathort, and travel north for ½ mile. Individuals, small or large groups welcome.

Admission £3.00

OPEN BY APPOINTMENT 1 MAY - 31 AUGUST 11am -7pm

Please telephone: 01577 840229 to arrange a visit.

40% to Strathcarron Hospice, Denny   60% net to SGS Charities

---

RENFREW & INVERCLYDE

Joint District Organisers: **Mrs J R Hutton,** Auchenclava, Finlaystone, Langbank PA14 6TJ

Mrs Daphne Ogg, Nittingshill, Kilmacolm PA13 4SG

Area Organisers: **Lady Denholm,** Newton of Bell Trees, Lochwinnoch PA12 4JL
Miss G Reynolds, 20 Calder Street, Lochwinnoch PA12 4EE
Mr J A Wardrop DL, St Kevins, Victoria Road, PaisleyPA2 9PT
PR - **Mrs G West,** Woodlands, 2 Birchwood Road, Uplawmoor,G78 4DG

Hon. Treasurer: **Mrs Jean Gillan,** Bogriggs Cottage, Carlung, West Kilbride KA23 9PS

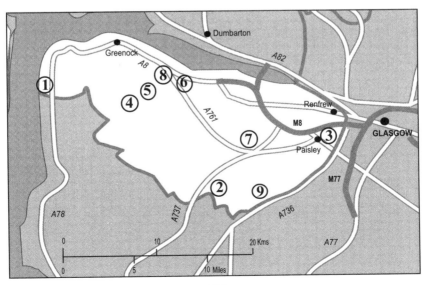

DATES OF OPENING

Ardgowan, Inverkip	Sunday 13 February	2 - 5pm
Auchengrange & Lochside, Lochwinnoch	Sunday 27 February	2 - 4pm
Finlaystone, Langbank	Sunday 17 April	2 - 5pm
Duchal, Kilmacolm	Sunday 15 May	2 - 5pm
Carruth, Bridge of Weir	Sunday 5 June	2 - 5pm
Uplawmoor Village Gardens	Sunday 19 June	2 - 6pm
Johnstone Gardens.	Sunday 10 July	2 - 5pm
Kilmacolm.	Sunday 31 July	1 - 5pm
Barshaw Park, Paisley	Sunday 7 August	2 - 5pm
SGS Plant Sale, Finlaystone, Langbank	Sunday 11 September	11.30am - 4pm

1. ARDGOWAN, Inverkip   ♿ (Not advisable if wet)

(Lady Shaw Stewart)
Woodland walks carpeted with snowdrops. (Strong waterproof footwear advised.) Tea in house. Snowdrop and plant stall, tombola and home produce. Inverkip 1½ miles. Glasgow/Largs buses in Inverkip.
Admission: £2.00 Children under 10 free
SUNDAY 13 FEBRUARY 2 - 5pm
40% to Ardgowan Hospice 60% net to SGS Charities

✿2. AUCHENGRANGE & LOCHSIDE, Lochwinnoch   ♿

Auchengrange (John and Jan Davies) **Lochside** (Keith and Kate Lough)
Two mature woodland gardens carpeted with snowdrops. Teas at Lochside. Stall at Auchengrange. Route: Auchengrange - From A737 at Lochwinnoch / Largs roundabout take Auchengrange Brae (heading south) well signed thereafter, short drive to entrance. Lochside - A737 200 yards east of Lochwinnoch / Largs roundabout. White railings on north side of road. Also direct access via RSPB Lochwinnoch Reserve.
Admission £3.00 (Includes both gardens) Children Free
SUNDAY 27 FEBRUARY 2 - 4pm
40% to Breast Cancer Care 60% net to SGS Charities

3. BARSHAW PARK - Walled Garden, Paisley   ♿ Gravel Paths

(Environmental Services Department, Renfrewshire Council)
Walled garden displaying colourful layout of summer bedding plants, herbaceous borders, mixed shrub borders containing plants suitable to touch and feel for the blind. Rose borders. Teas and Plant Stall. Route: from Paisley town centre along the Glasgow Road (A737) pass Barshaw Park and take first left into Oldhall Road & then first left again into walled garden car park. Pedestrian visitors can approach from Barshaw Park.
Admission by donation
SUNDAY 7 AUGUST 2 - 5pm
40% to Erskine Hospital 60% net to SGS Charities

4. CARRUTH, Bridge of Weir   ♿

(Mr & Mrs Charles Maclean)

Large Plant Sale including a wide selection of herbaceous, herbs, shrubs etc. Over 20 acres of long established rhododendrons, woodland and lawn gardens in lovely landscaped setting.Young arboretum. Home made teas. Access from B786 Kilmacolm/Lochwinnoch road or from Bridge of Weir via Torr Road.

Admission £2.50

SUNDAY 5 JUNE 2 - 5pm

40% to Cancer Relief Macmillan Fund 60% net to SGS Charities

---

5. DUCHAL, Kilmacolm   ♿

(The Lord and Lady Maclay)

18th century garden with walls particularly well planted and maintained, entered by footbridge over the Greenwater. Specie trees, hollies, old fashioned roses, shrubs and herbaceous borders with fruit orchards and vegetable garden. Lily pond. Loch and woodlands. Plant and produce stall. Home-made teas under cover. Kilmacolm 1 mile, B786. Greenock/Glasgow bus via Bridge of Weir; Knapps Loch stop is quarter mile from garden.

Admission £3.00 Children under 10 free

SUNDAY 15 MAY 2 - 5pm

20% to Ardgowan Hospice 20% to Strathcarron Hospice, Denny 60% net to SGS Charities

---

6. FINLAYSTONE, Langbank   ♿

(Mr & Mrs Arthur MacMillan)

Historic connection with John Knox and Robert Burns. Richly varied gardens with unusual plants overlooking the Clyde. A profusion of daffodils and early rhododendrons. Waterfalls & pond. Woodland walks with imaginative play and picnic areas. "Eye-opener" centre with shop. Doll Museum. Ranger service. Plant stall. Teas in the Celtic Tree in the walled garden.

Website: www.finlaystone.co.uk Tel: 01475 540285

On A8 west of Langbank, 10 minutes by car west of Glasgow Airport.

Admission £3.50 Children (under 4 free) & OAPs £2.50

SUNDAY 17 APRIL 2 - 5pm

40% to Quarrier's Village 60% net to SGS Charities

SUNDAY 11 SEPTEMBER SGS Special Plant Sale 11.30am - 4pm

An opportunity to purchase plants at the end of season clearance sale.

Finlaystone gardens and woodlands will be open as usual on this day.

40% of plant sales to Open Doors UK 60% net to SGS Charities

Why not look up the gardens on our website?
www.gardensofscotland.org
PHOTOS AND MAPS

❀ 7. JOHNSTONE GARDENS

Six well tended gardens each quite distinctive with much to interest the visitor:

1. 20 Hagg Road
  (Dan and Betty Logue)
2. 11 Hagg Road
  (Danny and Joan McLaughlin)
3. 23 Hagg Road
  (Yvonne and Jim Morris)

4. 19 Hagg Road
  (Mrs Florence Beacon).
5. 'Semmar' 34 Hagg Crescent
  (Flo and Archie Fraser)
6. 10 Bevan Grove
  (John and Agnes Kenny)

Teas and plant stall at garden no. 1. 20 Hagg Road

From High Street turn west into McDowall Street heading for Kilbarchan. Take north turn into Hagg Road at Graham Street / Kilbarchan Road junction. Well signposted thereafter.

Admission £3.00
SUNDAY 10 JULY 2 - 5pm
40% St. Vincent's Hospice   60% net to SGS Charities

---

8. KILMACOLM

1. Bellcroft - Gillburn Road
(Mr and Mrs K Graham)
A long garden with lawns, herbaceous borders, roses, shrubs and lawn. Next to St Fillans Church on Moss Road

2. The Bishops House - Porterfield Road
(Mr and Mrs P Yacoubian)
Rescued after many years of neglect, the garden is now a peaceful woodland and family friendly haven. A761 (Bridge of Weir road) right into Porterfield Road, 400 yards at top of hill on right.

3. Cloak - Cloak Road
(Mrs Inman and Mrs Murday)
Open after many years, a garden of about 3½ acres, including woodland garden, kitchen garden, herbaceous borders and a small pitch and putt course. Leave Kilmacolm by Finlaystone Road, continue out of village for 1 mile, turn left at stand of trees Cloak is near Auchendores resevoir. Alternative route via A761 heading Port Glasgow, right turn into Cloak Road.

4. High Mathernock, Auchentiber Road
(Mr and Mrs D Leslie)
Herbaceous garden with new (2004) Zen style area and water feature. Travel north on Port Glasgow Road (A761), turn left into Auchenbothie Road, then second left under bridge, continue for 1.2 miles.

5. Magdala- Port Glasgow Road
(Mr and Mrs Hughes)
Mixed herbaceous garden with interesting planting and views to Misty Law. Right hand side of Port Glasgow Road (A761) going north.

Teas at St Fillans Church, Moss Road Plant stall at Cloak.

A large map will be displayed at the centre of the village and hand maps will be available there and at all gardens, yellow signs along the way.

Admission £3.00 Children under 10 free
SUNDAY 31 JULY 1 - 5pm
40% Vet Aid   60% net to SGS Charities

---

9. UPLAWMOOR VILLAGE GARDENS   ♿   (partial)

A group of varied gardens at about 450ft above sea level in the small village of Uplawmoor, off the A736 Glasgow to Irvine Road, 5 miles southwest of Barrhead and 2miles north of Lugton. When entering the village from the northern (Barrhead) approach the gardens are in turn;

'WOODLANDS', Birchwood Road (Mr and Mrs J West)
A moderately sized garden with a small woodland area containing rhododendrons, azaleas and primulas: mixed borders with old-fasioned roses: greenhouse and fuschias.

'OCKLEY' 4 Tannoch Road (Miss J Rennie)
A garden with mixed planting in and 'old-fashioned' cottage garden style.

CHURCH MEMORIAL GARDEN Caldwell Parish Church, Neilston Road.

37 NEILSTON ROAD (Mr and Mrs D Ritson)
A garden with a wide variety of flowering shrubs, herbaceous plants, water feature and oriental garden.

11 NEILSTON ROAD (Miss A D Baker)
A sloping garden with shrubs, perennials, annual flowers and vegetables.

'GREYSTONES' Lochlibo Road (Mr and Mrs J Gauld)
A flower garden, a vegetable garden, herb garden and pond bordered with herbaceous plants.

Teas at the Mure Hall, Tannoch Road. Plant stall at Woodlands, Birchwood Road.
Admission £3.00 to include all gardens. Accompanied children under 14 free
SUNDAY 19 JUNE 2 - 6pm
40% to Accord Hospice 60% net to SGS Charities

Why not look up the gardens on our website?
www.gardensofscotland.org
PHOTOS AND MAPS

ROSS, CROMARTY, SKYE & INVERNESS

District Organiser: **Lady Lister-Kaye,** House of Aigas, Beauly IV4 7AD

Hon. Treasurer: **Mr Kenneth Haselock,** 2 Tomich, Strathglass, by Beauly IV4 7LZ

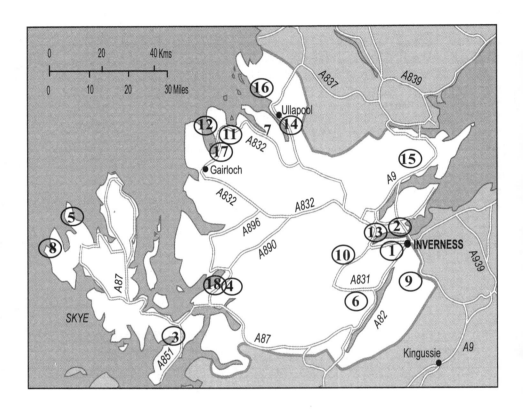

DATES OF OPENING

Abriachan, Loch Ness Side	February - November	9am - dusk
An Acarsaid, Ord, Isle of Skye	April - October	10am - 5.30pm
Attadale, Strathcarron	1 Apr - end Oct Closed Suns	10am - 5.30pm
Balmeanach House, Struan	Weds & Sats end Apr - mid Oct	11am - 4.30pm
Coiltie Garden, Divach, Drumnadrochit	14 May - 23 July	Noon - 7pm
Dunvegan Castle, Isle of Skye	21 March - 31 October	10am - 5.30pm
Leckmelm Shrubbery & Arboretum	1 April - 31 October	10am - 6pm
The Hydroponicum, Achiltibuie	March - 30 Sep & Mon - Fri in Oct	

Inverewe, Poolewe	Saturday 16 April	9.30am - 5pm
Dundonnell House, Dundonnell, by Garve	Wednesday 14 April	2 - 5pm
Allangrange, Munlochy	Sunday 8 May	2 - 5.30pm
The Hydroponicum, Achiltibuie	Sunday 15 May	10am - 6pm
Tullich, Strathcarron	Saturday 28 May	1 - 4.30pm
House of Gruinard, by Laide	Wednesday 1 June	2 - 5pm
Attadale, Strathcarron	Saturday 4 June	2 - 5pm
Dundonnell House, Dundonnell, by Garve	Wednesday 8 June	2 - 5pm
Allangrange, Munlochy	Sunday 12 June	2 - 5.30pm
Kilcoy Castle, Muir of Ord	Sunday 3 July	2 - 6pm
Novar, Evanton	Sunday 10 July	2.30pm
Glen Kyllachy, Tomatin	Sunday 31 July	2 - 6pm
House of Aigas & Field Centre, Beauly	Sunday 7 August	2 - 5.30pm
The Hydroponicum, Achiltibuie	Sunday 21 August	10am - 6pm
Inverewe, Poolewe	Sunday 11 September	9.30am - 5pm

1. ABRIACHAN GARDEN NURSERY, Loch Ness Side

(Mr & Mrs Davidson)

An outstanding garden. Over 4 acres of exciting plantings, with winding paths through native woodlands. Seasonal highlights – hellebores, primulas, meconopsis, hardy geraniums and colour-themed summer beds. Views over Loch Ness. New path to pond through the Bluebell Wood.

Admission £2.00.

FEBRUARY to NOVEMBER 9am - dusk

Donation to Scotland's Gardens Scheme

2. ALLANGRANGE, Munlochy, Black Isle &

(Major Allan Cameron)

A formal and a wild garden containing flowering shrubs, trees and plants, especially rhododendrons, shrub roses, meconopsis and primulas. Plants for sale. Exhibition of botanical paintings by Elizabeth Cameron. Tea & biscuits in house. Inverness 5 miles. Signposted off A9. Admission £2.00

SUNDAYS 8 MAY & 12 JUNE 2 - 5.30pm

20% to Highland Hospice 20% to Munlochy Village Hall 60% to SGS Charities

3. AN ACARSAID, Ord, Sleat, Isle of Skye

(Mrs Eileen MacInnes)

A two acre garden perched on low cliffs above the shore of Loch Eishort with stunning views to the Cuillins. Informal mixed plantings, started in the 1960s, with shrubbery and viewpoint, lawns, borders and scree bed and many cobbled paths. Route: Take A851 from Broadford or Armadale. Ord is signposted 5 miles from Armadale.

Admission By donation box

APRIL - OCTOBER 10am - 5.30pm

Donation to Crossroads Care & SGS Charities

4. ATTADALE, Strathcarron   ♿ (partial)

(Mr & Mrs Ewen Macpherson)
The Gulf Stream and surrounding hills and rocky cliffs create a microclimate for outstanding water gardens, old rhododendrons, unusual trees and fern collection in a geodesic dome. Japanese garden. Plants for sale. Tea room. On A890 between Strathcarron and South Strome.
Admission £3.00 Children £1.00   ♿ free
1 APRIL - end OCTOBER 10am - 5.30pm Closed Sundays
Donation to Scotland's Gardens Scheme
SATURDAY 4 JUNE 2 - 5pm Teas in house. Plant stall.
40% to The Highland Hospice 60% to SGS Charities

5. BALMEANACH HOUSE, Struan, Isle of Skye

(Mrs Arlene Macphie)
A formal garden with herbaceous border and bedding: and an azalea/rhododendron walk. To make this garden one third of an acre of croft land was fenced in during the late 1980s and there is now a woodland dell with fairies, three ponds and a shrubbery. Teas and Plant Stall. Route: A87 to Sligachan, turn left, Balmeanach is 5 miles north of Struan and 5 miles south of Dunvegan.
Admission By donation box - suggested donation - £2.00
WEDNESDAY & SATURDAYS END - APRIL - MID OCTOBER 11am - 4.30pm
40% to SSPCA 60% net to SGS Charities

6. COILTIE GARDEN, Divach, Drumnadrochit   ♿

(Gillian & David Nelson)
A wooded garden, an amalgamation of a Victorian flower garden abandoned 60 years ago and a walled field with a large moraine. This garden has been made over the past 15 years and development work is still in progress. Many trees, old and new, mixed shrub and herbaceous borders, roses, wall beds, rockery. No dogs please. Off A82 at Drumnadrochit. Take road signposted Divach uphill 2 miles. Past Divach Lodge, 150m.
Admission £2.00 Children free
OPEN DAILY 14 MAY - 23 JULY Noon - 7pm
40% to Amnesty International 60% to SGS Charities

7. DUNDONNELL HOUSE, Dundonnell by Garve   ♿

A 2000 year old yew tree is the centre of a formal walled garden. New borders compliment the existing camelias, rhododendrons, azaleas and the beautiful laburnum walk. There is also a riverside arboretum and woodland walk. No dogs please. Route: Off A832 between Braemore and Gairloch. Take Badralloch turn for 1 mile.
Admission £2.50 Children Free
WEDNESDAY 14 APRIL 2 - 5 pm - No Teas
WEDNESDAY 8 JUNE 2 - 5pm - Teas
40% to Tusk Trust 60% net to SGS Charities

8. DUNVEGAN CASTLE, Isle of Skye &

Dating from the 13th century and continuously inhabited by the Chiefs of MacLeod, this romantic fortress stronghold occupies a magnificent lochside setting. The gardens, originally laid out in the 18th century, have been extensively replanted and include lochside walks, woodlands and water gardens and a walled garden. Licensed restaurant. Two craft shops, woollen shop, kilts and country wear shop, clan exhibition, audio-visual theatre. Pedigree Highland cattle fold, boat trips to seal colony. Admission to Castle and Gardens: £6.80, students, OAPs & parties £5.80, children (5 -15) £3.80. Dunvegan village 1mile, 23 miles west of Portree.
Admission to Gardens only: £4.50 Children (5 - 15) £3.00
21 MARCH – 31st OCTOBER Mon—Sun 10am–5.30pm Last entry 5pm
Castle & Gardens November to Mid March Mon—Sun: 11am–4pm. Last entry 3.30pm
Donation to Scotland's Gardens Scheme

9. GLEN KYLLACHY, Tomatin &

(Mr & Mrs Philip Mackenzie)
Despite being sited at over eleven hundred feet there is a wide variety of trees, shrubs, rhododen-drons and herbaceous plants in borders around the house and large pond. Vegetable garden, polytunnel, conservatory, woodland walk and stunning views down a remote highland glen. Teas and home made goodies, well stocked plant stall. Route: turn of A9 at Tomatin, take Coignafearn and Garbole sungle track road along north side of River Findhorn - a cattle grid and gate on right after sign to Farr.
Admission £2.50 Children Free
SUNDAY 31 JULY 10am - 6pm
40%Local Charities   60% net to SGS Charities

10. HOUSE of AIGAS and FIELD CENTRE, by Beauly

(Sir John and Lady Lister-Kaye)
Aigas has a woodland walk overlooking the Beauly River with a collection of named Victorian specimen trees now being restored and extended with a garden of rockeries, herbaceous borders and shrubberies. Home made teas in house. Guided walks on nature trails: Route: 4½ miles from Beauly on A831 Cannich/Glen Affric road. No dogs please.
Admission from £3.00 Children free
SUNDAY 7 AUGUST 2 - 5.30pm
40% to Highland Hospice 60% net to SGS Charities

11. HOUSE OF GRUINARD, by Laide

(The Hon Mrs A G Maclay)
Hidden and unexpected garden developed in sympathy with stunning west coast estuary location. Wide variety of herbaceous and shrub borders with water garden and extended wild planting. Large choice of plants for sale. On A832 12 miles north of Inverewe and 9 miles south of Dundonnell. Teas.
Admission £2.00 Children under 16 free
WEDNESDAY 1 JUNE 2 - 5pm
40% to Highland Hospice 60% net to SGS Charities

12. INVEREWE, Poolewe &

(The National Trust for Scotland)

Magnificent 50-acre Highland garden, surrounded by mountains, moorland and sea-loch. Founded from 1862 by Osgood Mackenzie, it now includes a wealth of exotic plants, from Australian tree ferns to Chinese rhododendrons to South African bulbs. Shop and self-service restaurant. Plant sales.

Admission £8.00 (For further price information / concessions please see NTS advert at back of book)

SATURDAY 16 APRIL & SUNDAY 11 SEPTEMBER 9.30am - 5pm

40% to The Gardens Fund of the National Trust for Scotland   60% net to SGS Charities

---

13. KILCOY CASTLE, Muir of Ord &

(Mr & Mrs Nick McAndrew)

16th century castle (not open) surrounded by extensive terraced lawns, walled garden with fine herbaceous and shrub borders, surrounding vegetable garden. Woodland areas with rhododendrons, azaleas and particularly fine mature trees and shrubs. Teas. Plant Stall. Winner of "Inverness Courier" 'Large garden of the Year' award 2001 and 2002. Route: A9 to Tore roundabout, A832 signed Beauly and Muir of Ord. After 1½ miles, turn right at church signed Kilcoy, entrance is ½ mile on left.

Admission £2.50 Children under 12 free

SUNDAY 3 JULY 2 - 6pm

40% to Highland Hospice   60% net to SGS Charities

---

14. LECKMELM SHRUBBERY & ARBORETUM, by Ullapool

(Mr & Mrs Peter Troughton)

The restored 12 acre arboretum, planted in the 1870s, is full of splendid and rare trees, including 2 "Champions", specie rhododendrons, azaleas and shrubs. Warmed by the Gulf Stream, this tranquil woodland garden has alpines, meconopsis, palms, bamboos and winding paths which lead down to the sea.

Parking in walled garden.Situated by the shore of Loch Broom 3 miles south of Ullapool on the A835 Inverness/Ullapool road.

Admission £2.00 Children under 16 free

OPEN DAILY 1 APRIL - 31 OCTOBER 10am - 6pm

Donation to Scotland's Gardens Scheme and Local Charities

---

15. NOVAR, Evanton & (most areas)

(Mr & Mrs Ronald Munro Ferguson)

Water gardens with flowering shrubs, trees and plants, especially rhododendrons and azaleas. Large, five acre walled garden with formal 18th century oval pond (restored). New plantings since last year. Teas. Plant stall. Off B817 between Evanton and junction with A836; turn west up Novar Drive.

Admission £2.50 Children free

SUNDAY 10 JULY 2.30pm

40% to Diabetes UK   60% net to SGS Charities

16. THE HYDROPONICUM, Achiltibuie   ♿ (lower level)
(The Rt Hon Viscount Gough)
Situated as far north as Alaska, this pioneering indoor garden overlooks the beautiful Summer Isles. Personally guided tours of modern growing houses show a magnificent array of flowers, fruits, vegetables and herbs growing in 3 different climatic zones without either soil or pesticides.   Renewable energy exhibits, gift shop. Lilypond Cafe. Children's activities. Plant sales. Route: turn off A835 on to single track road to Achiltibuie and follow signs.
Admission £4.95 Children £2.95 Concessions £3.95 Family ticket £14.00
SUNDAYS 15 MAY AND 21 AUGUST 10am - 6pm
40% to R N L I   60% net to SGS Charities
Garden also open 21 March - October for further opening details see the advert at the back of the book.

---

17. TULLICH, Strathcarron
(Helene, Viscountess Scarsdale)
Beautifully situated in Wester Ross overlooking the sea of Loch Carron. The house and walled garden were built by prisoners after the '45. The garden and secret water garden were started in the 20th century. Many mature trees, specie rhododendrons, shrubs and herbaceous borders to see. There are short walks with wonderful views over the loch and hills. Teas. Plant stall. Route: Take the A890 from Achnasheen to Lochcarron, at the Strathcarron junction continue straight to Lochcarron A896, Tullich house is the first turning on the right after Heritage Centre.
Admission £2.00 Children £1.00
SATURDAY 28 MAY 1 - 4.30pm
40% to Save the Children (For Darfur)   60% net to SGS Charities

---

ROXBURGH

District Organiser:	**Mrs M D Blacklock,** Stable House, Maxton, St Boswells TD6 0EX
Area Organiser:	**Mrs T R Harley,** Estate house, Smailholm TD5 7PH
Hon. Treasurer:	**Mr Peter Jeary,** Kalemouth, Eckford, Kelso.

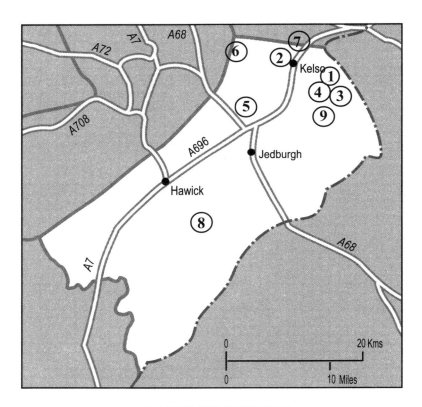

DATES OF OPENING

Floors Castle, Kelso .... Open daily from 3 Apr to 31 Oct 10am - 4.30pm

Monteviot, Jedburgh .... Sunday 12 June	2 - 5pm
Smailholm Village Gardens .... Sunday 26 June	2 - 6pm
Bracken Brae, Linton Downs, Kelso .... Sunday 3 July	2 - 6pm
Linton Bankhead Cottage, Morebattle .... Sunday 3 July	2 - 6pm
Meadowfield, Old Graden, Kelso .... Sunday 3 July	2 - 6pm
Rose Cottage, Eildon Village .... Sat & Sun 9 & 10 July	1 - 5pm
West Leas, Bonchester Bridge .... Sunday 17 July	2 - 6pm
Yetholm Village .... Sunday 7 August	2 - 6pm

114

1. BRACKEN BRAE, Linton Downs, Kelso   ♿

(Mr & Mrs Walter Thomson)

Small garden with charming collection of alpines, herbaceous and shrubs which fill a flower arrangers vase. Teas. Plant stall. Route: 6 miles from Kelso on B6436 to Morebattle.

JOINT OPENING With Meadow Field and Linton Bankhead Cottage

Admission £3.00 Children free (covers all 3 gardens)

SUNDAY 3 JULY 2 - 6pm

40% to Cancer Unit BGH NHS Trust 60% net to SGS Charities

---

2. FLOORS CASTLE, Kelso   ♿

(The Duke of Roxburghe)

The largest inhabited house in Scotland enjoys glorious views across rolling parkland, the River Tweed and the Cheviot Hills. Woodland garden, riverside and woodland walks, formal French style Millennium Parterre and the delightful walled garden. The walled garden contains spectacular herbaceous borders, vinery and peach house and in keeping with the tradition of a kitchen garden still supplies vegetables and soft fruit for the castle. Garden Centre, Children's Adventure Playground and a Coffee Shop specialising in homemade dishes prepared by the Duke's chef. 9 & 10 July - Gardener's Festival - Climbers and twiners

Admission: Walled Garden (honesty box)

Castle & Grounds: Adults £6.00 Seniors/Students £5.00 Children (5 - 16) £3.25 Under 5's free

Grounds & Gardens: Adults £3.00 Seniors/Students £1.50 Children (under 16) free

Walled Garden, Garden Centre and Coffee Shop OPEN DAILY ALL YEAR

Castle - Open daily from 25 March until 30 October 10am - 4.30pm

Enquiries 01573 223333 *www.floorscastle.com*

Donation to Scotland's Gardens Scheme

✿ 3. LINTON BANKHEAD COTTAGE, Morebattle   ♿

(Mr & Mrs Bruce Burton)

In 3 years an exceptional cottage garden has been created. Prolific vegetable beds and wonderful selection of fruit. Borders filled with colour. A bonsai collection grown from seed is sheltered by raised pond. This garden is enhanced by spectacular views. No dogs please.

JOINT OPENING With Meadow Field and Brackenbrae

Admission £3.00 Children free (covers all 3 gardens)

SUNDAY 3 JULY 2 - 6pm

40% to Cancer Unit BGH NHS Trust 60% net to SGS Charities

---

4. MEADOW FIELD, Old Graden, Kelso   ♿

(Mr & Mrs Roger Forster)

A new garden with herbaceous borders planted with perennials giving colour and material for flower aranging. Teas. Plant stall. Route: B6352 from Kelso to Yetholm

JOINT OPENING With Brackenbrae and Linton Bankhead Cottage

Admission £3.00 Children free (covers all 3 gardens)

SUNDAY 3 JULY 2 - 6pm

40% to Cancer Unit BGH NHS Trust 60% net to SGS Charities

---

5. MONTEVIOT, Jedburgh   ♿ (partially)

Monteviot garden lies along a steep rise above the Teviot valley, a setting which adds a sense of drama to its many outstanding features. From the box-hedged herb garden walk in front of the House with its unique and breathtaking view of the river below, down through the sheltered terraced rose-garden, into the River Garden originally designed in the 1960s by Percy Cane. Italianate in inspiration this garden slopes down between curved borders of herbaceous plants, shrubs, and roses to a broad stone landing stage. In the Water Garden, with its three islands linked by elegant curved wooden bridges, there is an interesting variety of bog and damp-loving plants with bamboo adding a sense of mystery. Open 1st April – 31st October daily 12 – 5pm. Turn off A68 three miles north of Jedburgh (B6400).
Admission £2.50 Children under 16 free
SUNDAY 12 JUNE 2 - 5pm Enquiries to (01835) 830380
Cream Teas in House; cakes, plants, tombola and The Jedburgh Instrumental Band.
20% to Riding for the Disabled Association, Border Group
20% to St Mary's Church, Jedburgh 60% net to SGS Charities

---

6. ROSE COTTAGE, Eildon Village   ♿

(Mrs Nancy Finlay)
The garden surrounding Rose Cottage is remarkable in many ways, offering the visitor a multitude of horticultural and visual treats. This 21st century new-built dwelling, forming part of a brilliantly planned small development in the existing village of Eildon, demonstrates how imaginative use of materials, informal planting schemes and sensitivity to the existing landscape can create a magical and productive garden space in less than five years. ABOVE ALL, THIS IS AN ORGANIC GARDEN WHERE NOTHING IS WASTED. Recycled plant material, well-rotted manure and effective companion planting ensure healthy yields of flowers, fruit and vegetables. Teas and Plant Stall.
Admission £1.50 Children free
SATURDAY & SUNDAY 9 & 10 JULY 1 - 5pm
40% to Henry Doubleday Research Association   60% net to SGS Charities

---

7. SMAILHOLM VILLAGE GARDENS   ♿ (some)

Smailholm provides a wealth of interest in several delightful gardens ranging in style and size from historic houses to traditional cottages. The village provides further interest with its imaginative recent developments, which include a wildlife pond and refurbished hall, with adjacent children's play area. In the hall the visitor can also admire the community's newly completed wallhanging depicting the village, while enjoying the delicious home made teas. Children can have fun in the play area.   Tickets and maps from the Village Hall. Teas. Plant stall. Route: B6397 between Kelso and Earlston.
Admission £2.50 Children free
SUNDAY 26 JUNE 2 - 6pm
40% to Smailholm Village Hall   60% net to SGS Charities

---

8. WEST LEAS, Bonchester Bridge ♿ (Partly)

(Mr and Mrs Robert Laidlaw)

The visitor to West Leas can share in the exciting and dramatic project on a grand scale still in the making. At its core is a passion for plants allied to a love and understanding of the land in which they are set. Collections of perennials and shrubs, many in temporary holding quarters, lighten up the landscape to magical effect. New landscaped water features, bog garden and extensive new shrub planting. A recently planted orchard, with underplantings of spring bulbs, demonstrates that the productive garden can be highly ornamental. Teas. Plant Stall.

Admission: £3.00   Children free

SUNDAY 17 JULY 2 - 6pm

40% to MacMillan Cancer Relief, Border Appeal 60% net to SGS Charities

---

9. YETHOLM VILLAGE

Situated at the north end of the Pennine Way and lying close to the Bowmont Water in the dramatic setting of the foothills of the Cheviots, the village of Town Yetholm offers visitors the chance to walk through several delightful gardens planted in a variety of styles and reflecting many distinctive horticultural interests. From newly established, developing and secret gardens to old and established gardens there is something here to interest everyone. The short walking distance between the gardens provides the added advantage of being able to enjoy the magnificence of the surrounding landscape to include 'Stacrough' and 'The Curr' which straddles both the Bowmont and Halterburn Valleys where evidence of ancient settlements remain. Tickets will be sold on the Village Green where there will be a produce stall to include plants, vegetables, jams and home baking. In adition at Almond Cottage a craft stall will offer examples of local wood turning, sketches and greeting cards. Home baked teas will also be served in the Youth Hall. Ample parking. Route: South of Kelso take the B6352 to Town Yetholm.

Admission £2.50, includes all gardens Children under 10 Free

SUNDAY 7 AUGUST 2 - 6pm

40% to RDA Borders 60% net to SGS Charities

STEWARTRY OF KIRKCUDBRIGHT

District Organiser: **Mrs C Cathcart,** Culraven, Borgue, Kirkcudbright DG6 4SG

Area Organisers: **Miss P M G Bain,** Annick Bank, Hardgate, Castle Douglas DG7 3LD

    Mrs A Chandler, Auchenvin, Rockcliffe, Dumfries DG5 4QQ

    Mrs W N Dickson, Chipperkyle, Kirkpatrick Durham,
       Castle Douglas DG7 3EY

    Mrs M R C Gillespie, Danevale Park, Crossmichael, Castle Douglas DG7 2LP

    Mrs J F Mayne, Hazelfield House, Auchencairn, Castle Douglas DG7 1RF

    Mrs W J McCulloch, Ardwall, Gatehouse of Fleet DG7 2EN

    Mrs Mary McIlvenna, Brae Neuk, Balmaclellan, Castle Douglas DG7 3QS

    Mrs C V Scott, 14 Castle Street, Kircudbright DG6 4JA

Hon. Treasurer: **Mr P Phillips,** The Old Manse, Old Ferry Road, Crossmichael
       Castle Douglas DG7 3AT

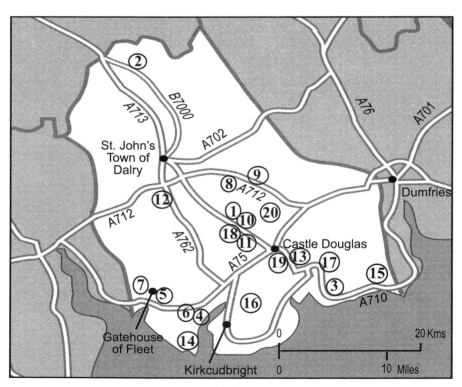

DATES OF OPENING

Barnhourie Mill, Colvend	May - Oct by appointment	
Carleton Croft, Borgue	July to August by appointment	
Danevale Park, Crossmichael	By appointment	
Southwick House, Dumfries	27 June - 1 July	

Danevale Park, Crossmichael	To be announced	
Senwick House, Brighouse Bay	Sunday 10 April	2 - 5pm
Walton Park, Castle Douglas	Sunday 1 May	2 - 5pm
Carstramont, Gatehouse of Fleet	Sunday 8 May	2 - 5pm
Stockarton, Kirkcudbright	Sunday 15 May	2 - 5pm
Corsock House, Castle Douglas	Sunday 29 May	2 - 5pm
Cally Gardens, Gatehouse of Fleet	Sunday 5 June	10am - 5.30pm
The Old Manse, Crossmichael	Sunday 12 June	2 - 5pm
19 Rhonepark Crescent, Crossmichael	Sunday 12 June	2 - 5pm
Southwick House, Dumfries	Sunday 26 June	2 - 5pm
Hensol, Mossdale	Sunday 3 July	2 - 5pm
Burnfoot, Borgue	Sunday 10 July	2 - 5pm
Millhouse, Rhonehouse	Sunday 17 July	2 - 5pm
The Mill House, Gelston	Sunday 17 July	2 - 5pm
Threave Garden, Castle Douglas	Sunday 24 July	9.30am - 5.30pm
Arndarroch Cottage, St John's Town of Dalry	Sunday 31 July	2 - 5pm
Crossmichael Gardens, Castle Douglas	Sunday 7 August	2 - 5pm
Cally Gardens, Gatehouse of Fleet	Sunday 14 August	10am - 5.30pm
Crofts, Kirkpatrick Durham	Sunday 21 August	2 - 5pm

1. 19 RHONEPARK CRESCENT, Crossmichael
(Pat and Geoff Packard)
Quarter acre garden on a south west facing slope. Extensive rockery, herbaceous border and mature conifers on three levels. Teas in Village Hall. Plants for sale. Village 3 miles north of Castle Douglas on the A713
JOINT OPENING WITH THE OLD MANSE , Crossmichael
Admission £3.00 Children Free
SUNDAY 12 JUNE 2 - 5pm
40% to Abbeyfield Stewartry Society Ltd (Bothwell House) 60% net to SGS Charities

2. ARNDARROCH COTTAGE, St John's Town of Dalry   ♿ (partly)
(Annikki and Matt Lindsay)
A young garden created since 1991 on a windswept hillside overlooking Kendoon Loch. A great variety of trees, some species roses and shrubs have been underplanted with herbaceous plants. Small pond and bog garden. A small kitchen garden. A new collection of oriental and medicinal plants. A small woodland was planted in 2000. The aim has been to create a semi-natural, wildlife friendly environment. Dogs on leads are welcome. About 5 miles from St John's Town of Dalry or from Carsphairn on the B7000. Parking at Kendoon Youth Hostel with lifts to the garden or you may enjoy the 1km walk.
Admission £3.00 Children Free
SUNDAY 31 JULY 2 - 5pm Teas and Plant Stall Garden quiz for children with small prizes.
Also open by appointment June to September Tel: 01644 460640
40% to Dumfries & Galloway Canine Rescue Centre   60% net to SGS Charities

3. BARNHOURIE MILL, Colvend   ♿ (partly)

(Dr M R Paton)
Flowering shrubs and trees, dwarf conifers and an especially fine collection of rhododendron species. Cars free. Dalbeattie 5 miles. Route A710 from Dumfries.
Admission £3.00 Children free
MAY - OCTOBER by appointment for groups and individuals. Tel: 01387 780269
40% to Scottish Wildlife Trust 60% net to SGS Charities

❀ 4. BURNFOOT, Borgue

(Mrs Jean Severn)
Pretty cottage garden in coastal setting with small spring-fed pond surrounded by a 'friends' flower border. Young extensive pergola, newly created woodland garden descending to a tumbling burn. Teas and plant stall. Dogs very welcome on leads. 3 miles from Kircudbright on B727. Parking at The Dhoon Beach
Admission £3.00 Children Free
SUNDAY 10 JULY 2- 5pm
40% Dumfries & Galloway Canine Rescue Centre 60% net to SGS Charities

5. CALLY GARDENS, Gatehouse of Fleet   ♿

(Mr Michael Wickenden)
A specialist nursery in a fine 2.7 acre, 18th century walled garden with old vinery and bothy, all surrounded by the Cally Oak woods. Our collection of 3,500 varieties can be seen and a selection will be available pot-grown, especially rare herbaceous perennials. Forestry nature trails nearby. Route: From Dumfries take the Gatehouse turning off A75 and turn left, through the Cally Palace Hotel Gateway from where the gardens are well signposted. Admission charge: £2.50. Open Easter Saturday – last Sunday in September: Tues–Frid 2–5.30pm, Sat & Sun 10am–5.30pm. Closed Mondays.
SUNDAYS 5 JUNE & 14 AUGUST 10am - 5.30pm
40% to Save the Children Fund 60% net to SGS Charities

6. CARLETON CROFT, Borgue   ♿

(Mr and Mrs D J Hartley)
Small cottage garden with well stocked herbaceous beds, shrubs, trees, tubs and baskets.
Created for wildlife and the pleasure of gardening. On the B272 between Borgue and Gatehouse of Fleet. Teas and plant stall.
Admission by donation
OPEN BY APPOINTMENT JULY TO AUGUST daylight hours Tel: 01557 870 447
40% to Wigtownshire Animal Welfare Association 60% net to SGS Charities

7. CARSTRAMONT, Gatehouse of Fleet   ♿ (partly)

(Mrs Robin Dean)
A new garden with rhododendrons and azaleas. Woodland walks. Teas. On entering Gatehouse off A75 turn right to Lauriston, after ¾ mile turn left and follow arrows.
Admission £3.00 Children Free
SUNDAY 8 MAY 2 - 5pm
40% to Macmillan Cancer Relief 60% net to SGS Charities

8. CORSOCK HOUSE, Castle Douglas

(Mr & Mrs M L Ingall)

Rhododendrons, woodland walks with temples , water gardens and loch. David Bryce turretted "Scottish Baronial" house in background. A limited selection of plants for sale. Teas. Cars free. Dumfries 14 miles, Castle Douglas 10 miles, Corsock half mile on A712.

SUNDAY 29 MAY 2 - 5pm

Also open by appointment: Tel. 01644 440250

40% to Corsock & Kirkpatrick Durham Kirk 60% net to SGS Charities

---

9. CROFTS, Kirkpatrick Durham   ♿ (partly)

(Mr & Mrs Andrew Dalton)

Victorian garden in the process of renovation and extension. Teas. Plant stall. A75 to Crocketford, then 3 miles on A712.

Admission £3.00 Children Free.

SUNDAY 21 AUGUST 2 - 5pm

40% to Corsock & Kirkpatrick Durham Church 60% net to SGS Charities

---

10. CROSSMICHAEL GARDENS - Joint Opening

3 MAIN STREET, Crossmichael

(K Hutchison)

Well established flower arranger's garden with many unusual plants. Plant stall.

5 MAIN STREET, Crossmichael

(Mrs Jeanie Galloway)

Small village garden with a mixture of perennials and annuals. Plant stall.

19 RHONEPARK CRESCENT, Crossmichael

(Pat and Geoff Packard)

Extensive rockery, herbaceous border and mature conifers on 3 levels.

SQUARE POINT, Crossmichael Road

(Lt Col E W Jenno)

Small garden of roughly two thirds of an acre, put down entirely to beds and borders. Contains hundreds of different shrubs and perennial plants hardy in this area.

On A713 1½ miles from Crossmichael, then signed.

Admission £3.00 Children Free   Teas in Village Hall.

SUNDAY 7 AUGUST 2 - 5pm

40% to Galloway Mountain Rescue 60% net to SGS Charities

---

11. DANEVALE PARK, Crossmichael

(Mrs M R C Gillespie)

Open for snowdrops. Mature garden with woodland walks alongside the River Dee. Walled garden. Tea in house. Route: A713. Crossmichael 1 mile, Castle Douglas 3 miles.

Admission £3.00 Children Free

DATE for Snowdrops - TO BE ANNOUNCED

Also open by appointment till 1 June Tel:01556 670223

40% to Crossmichael Village Hall 60% net to SGS Charities

---

12. HENSOL, Mossdale, Castle Douglas &

(Lady Henderson)
An early 19th century granite house designed by Lugar. Established garden surrounding house.
Alpines and woodland garden. Museum of artefacts in use 100 years ago.
River walk. Plant stall. Cars free. Tea in house £2.00. Route: Between Ringford on A75 and New
Galloway on the A762, 3 miles north of Laurieston.
Admission £3.00 Children Free
SUNDAY 3 JULY 2 - 5pm
40% to RNLI 60% net to SGS Charities

---

13. MILLHOUSE, Rhonehouse

(Bill Hean)
Small garden. Mainly herbaceous and alpines. Vegetable garden. Signs in village of Rhonehouse,
just off A75 west of Castle Douglas.
Admission £3.00 Children Free
JOINT OPENING WITH THE MILL HOUSE GELSTON
SUNDAY 17 JULY 2 - 5pm
All takings to SGS Charities

---

14. SENWICK HOUSE, Brighouse Bay &

(Mrs Geraldine Austin)
Georgian country house set in 10 acres of mature gardens with splendid views of Brighouse Bay.
Magnificent daffodil display with over 300 different varieties. Gardens feature mature trees,
conifers, shrubs and woodland. Route: from Kirkcudbright take the B727 to Borgue and follow
signs to Brighouse Bay. Cream teas.
Admission £3.00 Children Free
SUNDAY 10 APRIL 2 - 5pm
40% to Macmillan Cancer Relief 60% net to SGS Charities

---

15. SOUTHWICK HOUSE, Southwick &

(Mr & Mrs R H L Thomas)
Traditional formal walled garden with lily ponds, herbaceous borders, shrubs, vegetables, fruit
and greenhouses. Fine trees and lawns through which flows the Southwick burn. New
developments in water garden. Teas. On A710 near Caulkerbush. Dalbeattie 7 miles, Dumfries
17 miles.
Admission £3.00 Children free
SUNDAY 26 JUNE 2 - 5pm
ALSO OPEN MONDAY 27 JUNE - FRIDAY 1 JULY - Honesty Box
40% to Perennial (GRBS) 60% net to SGS Charities

---

16. STOCKARTON, Kirkcudbright &

(Lt Col & Mrs Cliff)
A garden begun in 1994. Our aim has been to create informal and small gardens around a
Galloway farmhouse, leading down to a lochan. Teas. Exciting plant stall. On B727
Kirkcudbright/Gelston road; 3 miles from Kirkcudbright, 7 miles from Castle Douglas.
Admission £3.00 Children Free
SUNDAY 15 MAY 2 – 5pm
40% to Loch Arthur Community 60% net to SGS Charities

17. THE MILL HOUSE, Gelston
(Magnus Ramsay)
A collection of plants for small gardens. Route: Entrance to village of Gelston from Castle Douglas at the 30 mph speed limit sign on B727.
Admission £3.00 Children Free
JOINT OPENING WITH MILLHOUSE RHONEHOUSE
SUNDAY 17 JULY 2 - 5pm
40% to Afghan Schools Trust 60% net to SGS Charities

---

18. THE OLD MANSE, Crossmichael ♿
(Mr and Mrs Peter Phillips)
Roses, shrubs, azaleas, herbaceous, rock garden in a constantly developing working garden created over the past decade. Splendid views to River Dee. Sale plants all from our own stock. Teas in Crossmichael Village Hall.
JOINT OPENING WITH 19 RHONEPARK CRESCENT, Crossmichael
Admission £3.00 Children Free
SUNDAY 12 JUNE 2 - 5pm
40% to Abbeyfield Stewartry Society Ltd (Bothwell House) 60% net to SGS Charities

---

19. THREAVE GARDEN, Castle Douglas ♿
(The National Trust for Scotland)
Home of the Trust's School of Practical Gardening. Spectacular daffodils in spring, colourful herbaceous borders in summer, striking autumn trees and heather garden. Plant centre. Route: A75, one mile west of Castle Douglas.
Admission £6.00 Children & OAPs £4.75 Family £14.50
SUNDAY 24 JULY 9.30am - 5.30pm
40% to The Gardens Fund of The National Trust for Scotland 60% net to SGS Charities

---

20. WALTON PARK, Castle Douglas
(Mr Jeremy Brown)
Walled garden, gentian border. Flowering shrubs, rhododendrons and azaleas. Cars free. Teas. Plant stall. Route: B794 to Corsock, 3½ miles from A75.
Admission £3.00 Children Free
SUNDAY 1 MAY 2 - 5pm
40% to Corsock & Kirkpatrick Durham Church 60% net to SGS Charities

---

Why not look up the gardens on our website?
www.gardensofscotland.org
PHOTOS AND MAPS

STIRLING

Joint District Organisers: **Maud Crawford**, St Blane's House, Dunblane FK15 OER
Lesley Stein, Southwood, Southfield Crescent, Stirling FK8 2JQ

Area Organisers: **Carola Campbell**, Kilbryde Castle, Doune FK15 3HN

Jean Gore, Braehead, 69 Main Street, Doune FK16 8BW

Jane Hutchison, Settie, Kippen FK8 3HN

Fleur McIntosh, 8 Albert Place, Stirling FK8 2QL

Sue Stirling-Aird, Old Kippenross, Dunblane FK15 OCQ

Helen Younger, Old Leckie, Gargunnock FK8 3BN

Hon. Treasurer **John McIntyre**, 18 Scott Brae, Kippen FK8 3DL

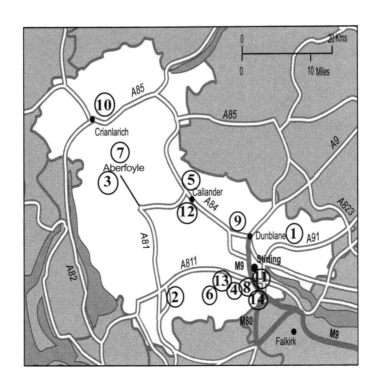

DATES OF OPENING

14 Glebe Crescent, Tillicoultry	....	By appointment
Ballindalloch, Balfron	....	By appt May and June
Callander Lodge, Callander	....	By appointment
Camallt, Fintry	....	By appointment
Daldrishaig House, Aberfoyle	....	By appointment
Gargunnock House, Gargunnock	....	Wednesdays mid April -
	....	mid June & in Sept & Oct
	....	and By appointment
Kilbryde Castle, Dunblane	....	By appointment

The Pass House, Kilmahog	Sunday 24 April	2 - 5pm
Touch, Stirling	Sunday 24 April	2 - 5pm
Brioch, Kippen	Sunday 1 May	2 - 5pm
Southwood Gardeners' Market, Stirling	Sunday 8 May	1 - 5pm
Kilbryde Castle, Dunblane	Sunday 15 May	2 - 5pm
Blairuskin Lodge, Kinlochard	Sunday 22 May	2 - 5pm
Gargunnock House, Gargunnock	Sunday 22 May	2 - 5pm
The Pass House, Kilmahog	Sunday 29 May	2 - 5pm
14 Glebe Crescent, Tillicoultry	Sunday 5 June	1 - 5pm
Lochdochart, Crianlarich	Sunday 5 June	12 - 4pm
Kilbryde Castle, Dunblane	Sunday 19 June	2 - 5pm
Thorntree, Arnprior	Sunday 26 June	2 - 5pm

1. 14 GLEBE CRESCENT, Tillicoultry &

(Jim & Joy McCorgray)

Half acre beautifully designed plantsman's garden with specialist areas. Japanese, ornamental grasses, bonsai, conifer and perfumed gardens. Koi carp pool. Woodland area in spring offers paticular interest. As featured on 'The Beechgrove garden' and in 'Gorgeous Gardens ' and 'Garden Answers' magazines. Home made teas. Good selection of home grown plants for sale. Route: A91 St Andrews/Stirling road; east end of Tillicoultry; yellow arrow at Glebe Crescent. Admission £2.50 Senior Citizens £1.50 Children Free

SUNDAY 5 JUNE 1 - 5pm

Also by appointment. Tel: 01259 750484

40% to The New Struan School for Autism Appeal 60% net to SGS Charities

2. BALLINDALLOCH, Balfron &

(Mr and Mrs A M M Stephen)

On the site of an earlier castle, a Victorian country house was dramatically reduced around 1980 and the gardens replanned for present day maintenance. Paved terraces and ruin garden with 17th C obelisk sundial. Rhododendrons, other shrubs, specimen trees and perennials include recent plantings amid lawns and a small wooded glen. Views of Campsie Fells. Route: A875 between Killearn and Balfron.

Admission Adults £2.50 - Coffee, tea and historical exhibition available.

OPEN BY APPOINTMENT MAY & JUNE TEL: 01360 440202

Donation to Scotland's Gardens Scheme

3. BLAIRUSKIN LODGE, Kinlochard
(Mr & Mrs D Miller)

Flowering shrubs, rhododendrons, woodland walk, vegetable garden, small cottage garden. Teas. Plant stall. Cake stall. Route: A81 Glasgow/Aberfoyle; 6 miles from Aberfoyle on Inversnaid Road, one mile from Forest Hills. Parking at Kinlochard Village Hall with free minibus service. Admission £2.50 Children under 12 free

SUNDAY 22 MAY 2 – 5pm
20% to Matthew Miller Cancer Fund   20% to St Mary's Episcopal Church, Aberfoyle 60% net to SGS Charities

---

✿4. BRIOCH, Kippen   ♿
(Sir Peter and Lady Hutchison)

Large woodland garden, rhododendrons many special trees and famous Yew. Victorian walk along burn, small waterfall and attractive bridges. Walled garden under restoration. Dogs on leads please. Teas. Route: Loop road to Kippen off A811 one mile west of Kippen Cross. Admission £2.50 Children Free

SUNDAY 1 MAY 2 - 5pm - (Talk at 3.30pm)
40% to The Younger (Benmore) Trust   60% net to SGS Charities

---

5. CALLANDER LODGE, Leny Feus, Callander
(Miss Caroline Penney)

Victorian garden laid out in 1863. Four acres of mature trees, shrubs, herbaceous and rose borders. Waterfall pool. Fern grotto. Bog garden and water garden. Woodland walk. Vegetable garden. Route: A84 west through Callander, turn right at sign for Leny Feus. Garden is at end on left. Admission £2.50

BY APPOINTMENT. Tel: 01877 330 136
40% to Camphill Blair Drummond Trust   60% net to SGS Charities

---

6. CAMALLT, Fintry   ♿ (partly)
(Rebecca East and William Acton)

8 acre garden previously open for its old and interesting daffodil cultivars dating from 1600 which carpet the woodland beside waterfalls and burn, at their best during early April. These are followed by bluebells, rhododendrons and azaleas. Herbaceous teraced gardens under continued progression of change meet lawns which run down to the Endrick Water. Other features include ponds and bog garden still under development. No dogs. Route: from Fintry Village B822 to Lennoxtown, approx. 1 mile then turn left to Denny on B818, Camallt entrance on right. Admission £2.50 Children Free

OPEN ALL YEAR BY APPOINTMENT - monitored telephone answering machine 01360 860075
40% to The Menzies Hall Building Project 60% net to SGS Charities

7. DALDRISHAIG HOUSE, Aberfoyle

(John and Fiona Blanche)

A fascinating garden in a spectacular setting on the banks of Loch Ard. Formal front garden, also rock, gravel and bog gardens, even a cliff. New raised vegetable beds (ever so small) from where more rhodies have been cleared. Disabled parking only. Free mini-bus from Aberfoyle car park - 5 minutes.

Admission £3.00 Children free

SUNDAY 12 JUNE 2 - 5pm

GROUPS WELCOME BY APPOINTMENT Tel: 01877 382223

40% to Aberfoyle Parish Church 60% net to SGS Charities

---

8. GARGUNNOCK HOUSE, Gargunnock &

(Gargunnock Trustees)

Five acres of mature rhododendrons, azaleas, unusual flowering shrubs and wonderful trees with glorious autumn colour. Good plant sale all year. Dogs on lead please. Route: 5miles west of Stirling on A811.

Admission Adults £2.50 Children Free

SUNDAY 22 MAY 2 - 5pm

AND <u>WEDNESDAYS</u> FROM MID APRIL - MID JUNE & IN SEPT & OCT 2 - 5pm

Also By Appointment Tel: 01786 860392

40% to Childrens Hospice Association (Scotland)   60% net to SGS Charities

---

9. KILBRYDE CASTLE, Dunblane, Perthshire   & (partly)

(Sir James & Lady Campbell & Jack Fletcher)

Traditional Scottish baronial house rebuilt 1877 to replace building dating from 1461. Partly mature gardens with additions and renovations since 1970. Lawns overlooking Ardoch Burn with wood and water garden. Three miles from Dunblane and Doune, off the A820 between Dunblane and Doune. On Garden Scheme days, signposted from A820. No dogs.

Admission £2.50 Accompanied children under 16 and OAPs £2.00

SUNDAY 15 MAY 2 - 5pm - No Teas

SUNDAY 19 JUNE 2 - 5pm - Teas + Toilets

Also by appointment. Tel: 01786 824897

40% to Leighton Library, Strathcarron Hospice 60% net to SGS Charities

---

10. LOCHDOCHART, Crianlarich   &

(John & Seona Christie of Lochdochart)

Walled garden – fruit, flowers and vegetables. Mature policy woods - rhododendrons and azaleas. Picnic beach by Loch Iubhair. Plant and produce stall. Bring your picnic lunch. No dogs please. Route: A85, 4 miles east of Crianlarich. Stone pillars on north side of road.

Admission £3.00 Children free

SUNDAY 5 JUNE 12 - 4pm

40% to Cancer Relief Macmillan Fund 60% net to SGS Charities

---

11. SOUTHWOOD GARDENERS' MARKET, Southfield Crescent, Stirling ♿

(John & Lesley Stein)
New town garden redesigned in 1987. ¾ acre of mixed planting including new lavander bed.
Home baking stall. Cream Teas. Full range of gardeners' stalls. Route: Kings Park Avenue and
Snowdon Place, signed from Carlton Cinema, Drummond Place and St. Ninians Road.
Admission £3.00   Children free
SUNDAY 8 MAY 1 - 5pm
40% to Strathcarron Hospice   60% net to SGS Charities

12. THE PASS HOUSE, Kilmahog, Callander ♿ (partly)

(Dr & Mrs D Carfrae)
Well planted medium sized garden with steep banks down to swift river. Camellias,
rhododendrons, azaleas, alpines and shrubs. Teas and plant stall on 29 May only.
2 miles from Callander on A84 to Lochearnhead.
Admission £2.50 Children free
SUNDAYS 24 APRIL & 29 MAY 2 - 5pm
40% to Crossroads Care Attendant Scheme 60% net to SGS Charities

13. THORNTREE, Arnprior ♿

(Mark & Carol Seymour)
Charming small cottage garden with flower beds around courtyard. Apple walk, fern garden and
Saltire garden. Lovely views from Ben Lomond to Ben Ledi. Cream teas. Plant stall. Cake
stall. No dogs please. Route: A811. In Arnprior take Fintry Road, Thorntree is second on right.
Admission £2.50 Children free
SUNDAY 26 JUNE 2 - 5pm
40% Bannockburn Group RDA 60% net to SGS Charities

14. TOUCH, Stirling

(Angus Watson)
Exceptionally fine Georgian House (House also open £1.50). Walled garden with herbaceous
and shrub borders, specie and dwarf rhododendrons, magnolias and interesting shrubs.
Woodland walk. Small plant stall. Teas. Route: West from Stirling on A811 then take
Cambusbarron Road.
Admission £2.00 Children free
SUNDAY 24 APRIL 2 - 5pm
40% Strathcarron Hospice 60% net to SGS Charities

TWEEDDALE

District Organiser:	**Mrs Tricia Kennedy,** Newhall, Carlops EH26 9LY
Area Organisers:	**Mrs D Balfour-Scott,** Dreva Craig, Broughton, Biggar ML12 6HH
	Mr K St. C Cunningham, Hallmanor, Peebles EH45 9JN
	Mrs H B Marshall, Baddinsgill, West Linton, EH46 7HL
Hon. Treasurer:	**Mr J Birchall,** Drumelzier Old Manse, Drumelzier, Broughton, By Biggar ML12 6JD

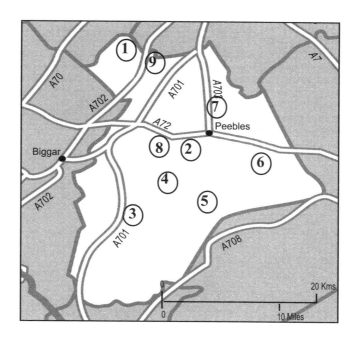

DATES OF OPENING

Kailzie Gardens, Peebles .... Open all year round

Barns, Kirkton Manor	Sunday 17 April	2 - 5pm
Stobo Water Garden, Stobo	Friday 27 May	11am - 4pm
Hallmanor, Peebles..	Sunday 29 May	2 - 6pm
Baddingsgill, West Linton	Sunday 12 June	2 - 5pm
Broughton Place Stable Cottages, Broughton	Sunday 12 June	2 - 5pm
West Linton Village Gardens.	Sunday 24 July	2 - 5pm
Portmore, Eddleston	Sunday 31 July	2 - 5pm
Broughton Place Stable Cottages, Broughton	Sunday 4 September	10am - 6pm
Dawyck Botanic Garden, Stobo	Sunday 4 September	10am - 6pm

---

⊕1. BADDINSGILL, West Linton   ♿   (limited access)
(Gavin and Elaine Marshall)
Beautiful woodland garden 1,000 ft up in the Pentland Hills above West Linton. Stunning
situation. Woodland and riverside walks. Bluebells, azaleas and rhododendrons. Water garden.
Teas and plant stall. Route: A702 to West Linton uphill past golf course.
Admission £2.50 Children Free
SUNDAY 12 JUNE 2 - 5pm
40% to Multiple Sclerosis Society Scotland   60% net to SGS Charities

2. BARNS, Kirkton Manor   ♿ (partially)

(Elizabeth & David Benson)

The property is the setting for John Buchan's 'John Burnet of Barns'. Late 16th century (recently restored) peel tower and 1773 house with stable block set in an extensive area of snowdrops and daffodils on the Tweed. Fledgeling arboretum. We hope to have the Tower open for guided viewing for the first time (additional charge). Teas. Route: Turn off the A72 to Kirkton Manor for 1½ miles; turn right into 1 mile drive. Parking near house.

Admission £2.50   Children Free

SUNDAY 17 APRIL 2 - 5pm

40% to Manor & Lyne Church   60 % net to SGS Charities

✿3. BROUGHTON PLACE STABLE COTTAGES, Broughton   ♿ (very limited)

(David Binns and Liz Hanson)

Small garden at 800ft above sea level created from a field site since 1995 by David and Liz and packed with a most wonderful selection of plants both interesting and unusual.: Well known favourites e.g. meconopsis sheldonii, Primulas, Rogersias, Cyanthus lobatus, a Thyme scree, a blue and white garden and probably the only dwarf grand fir in the country plus some unusual Scottish natives e.g. a form of Salix endemic to St. Kilda. A 4,500 year old bog root sculpture amongst others. Plant stall. Teas available locally. Route: Off A701 turn uphill towards Broughton Gallery.

Admission £2.50   Children Free

SUNDAY 12 JUNE 2 - 5pm

SUNDAY 4 SEPTEMBER 10am - 6pm

40% to SSPCA   60% net to SGS Charities

---

4. DAWYCK BOTANIC GARDEN, Stobo   ♿ (limited access)

(Regional Garden of the Royal Botanic Garden Edinburgh and one of the National Botanic Gardens of Scotland)

Stunning collection of rare trees and shrubs. With over 300 years of tree planting Dawyck is a world famous arboretum with mature specimens of Chinese conifers, Japanese maples, Brewer's spruce, the unique Dawyck Beech and Sequoiadendrons from North America which are over 45 metres tall. Bold herbaceous plantings run along the burn. Range of trails and walks. Conservatory shop with plant sales, coffees and teas. Guide dogs only. Route: 8 miles south west of Peebles on B712.

Admission £3.50   Concessions £3.00   Children £1.00   Families £8.00

SUNDAY 4 SEPTEMBER 10am - 6pm

Donation to Scotland's Gardens Scheme

---

5. HALLMANOR, Kirkton Manor, Peebles   ♿ (partially)

(Mr & Mrs K St C Cunningham)

Rhododendrons and azaleas, primulas, wooded grounds with loch and salmon ladder. Set in one of the most beautiful valleys in the Borders. Teas. Plant stall. Peebles 6 miles. Off A72 Peebles/Glasgow road. Follow SGS signs.

Admission £2.50   Children free

SUNDAY 29 MAY 2 - 6pm

40% to Manor & Lyne Church   60% net to SGS Charities

---

6. KAILZIE GARDENS, Peebles &

(Lady Buchan-Hepburn)
Semi-formal walled garden, with shrub and herbaceous borders. Rose garden. Well stocked greenhouses. Woodland and burnside walks among massed spring bulbs, rhododendrons and azaleas. The garden is set among fine old trees and includes the old larch planted in 1725. Free car park. Picnic area. Children's play area. Shop. Tearoom / licensed restaurant. 18 Hole putting green. Stocked trout pools. Visit the 'Osprey Watch' live CCTV beamed to a visitor centre. $2\frac{1}{2}$ miles east of Peebles on B7062.

OPEN ALL YEAR ROUND
10am - 5.30pm Children under 5 free

26 March - 31 June 11am - 5.30pm	Adults £2.50	Children 75p
June 1 - end October	Adults £3.00	Children £1.00
End October - March 25	Adults £2.00	

Donation to Scotland's Gardens Scheme

---

7. PORTMORE, Eddleston & (partially)

(Mr & Mrs D H L Reid)
Herbaceous borders. Herb garden. Ornamental vegetable garden. Greenhouse with Victorian grotto. Shrub rose garden and parterre. Cream teas. Plant stall. Dogs on lead please. Edinburgh to Peebles bus No.62.
Admission £2.50
SUNDAY 31 JULY 2 - 5pm
40% to Kulika in Uganda   60% net to SGS Charities

---

8. STOBO WATER GARDEN, Stobo, Peebles

(Mr Hugh Seymour and Mr Charles Seymour)
Water garden, lakes and rhododendrons. Woodland walks. Cars free. Teas locally. Dogs on a lead please. Peebles 7 miles, signposted on B712 Lyne/Broughton road.
Admission £2.50 Children Free
FRIDAY 27 MAY 11am - 4pm
40% to Fergus Maclay Leukaemia Trust 60% net to SGS Charities

---

9. WEST LINTON VILLAGE GARDENS & (partially)

A group of village gardens: cottage style, plantsman's and a secret courtyard showing iris, hostas, delphiniums, campanulas, hardy geraniums, rogersias, flox, many more hardy perennials, shrubs and conifers. Route: A701 or A702 and follow signs. Tickets, maps, teas and plant stall in New Church Hall in the centre of the village.
Admission £3.00 includes all gardens. Children Free
SUNDAY 24 JULY 2 - 5pm
20% to Ben Walton Trust   20% to Breast Cancer Fund, Borders General Hospital
60% net to SGS Charities

WIGTOWN

District Organiser: **Mrs Francis Brewis,** Ardwell House, Stranraer DG9 9LY

Area Organisers: **Mrs V WolseleyBrinton,** Chlenry, Castle Kennedy,
Stranraer DG9 8SL
Mrs Andrew Gladstone, Craichlaw, Kirkcowan,
Newton Stewart DG8 0DQ

Hon. Treasurer: **Mr G Fleming,** Ardgour, Stoneykirk, Stranraer DG9 9DL

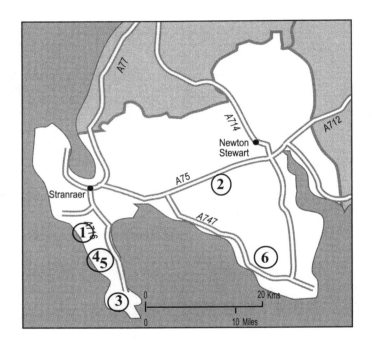

DATES OF OPENING

Ardwell House Gardens, Ardwell .... Daily 1 April - 30 September	10am - 5pm
Logan House Gardens, Port Logan .... Daily 1 February - 1 April	10am - 4pm
2 April - 31 August	9am - 6pm
Logan House Gardens, Port Logan .... Sunday 1 May	9am - 6pm
Woodfall Gardens, Glasserton .... Sunday 15 May	2 - 5.30pm
Damnaglaur House, Drummore .... Sunday 22 May	2 - 5pm
Logan Botanic Garden, Port Logan .... Sunday 29 May	10am - 6pm
Damnaglaur House, Drummore .... Sunday 26 June	2 - 5pm
Woodfall Gardens, Glasserton .... Sunday 3 July	2 - 5.30pm
Craichlaw, Kirkcowan .... Sunday 14 August	2 - 5pm

1. ARDWELL HOUSE GARDENS, Ardwell, Stranraer
(Mr & Mrs Francis Brewis)
Daffodils, spring flowers, rhododendrons, flowering shrubs, coloured foliage and rock plants. Moist garden at smaller pond and a walk round larger ponds, with views over Luce Bay. Plants for sale and self-pick fruit in season. Collecting box. House not open. Dogs welcome on leads. Picnic site on shore. Stranraer 10 miles. Route A76 towards Mull of Galloway.
Admission £3.00 Concessions £2.00 Children under 14 free
DAILY 1 APRIL - 30 SEPTEMBER 10am - 5pm
Donation to Scotland's Gardens Scheme

2. CRAICHLAW, Kirkcowan ♿
(Mr & Mrs Andrew Gladstone)
Formal garden around the house, with herbaceous borders. Set in extensive grounds with lawns, lochs and woodland. A path around the main loch leads to a water garden returning past an orchard of old Scottish apple varieties. Teas. Plant stall. Signposted off A75, 8 miles west of Newton Stewart and B733, one mile west of Kirkcowan.
Admission £2.50 Accompanied children under 14 free
SUNDAY 14 AUGUST 2 - 5pm
40% to Kirkcowan Parish Church   60% net to SGS Charities

3. DAMNAGLAUR HOUSE, Drummore
(Mr & Mrs E Collins)
Small landscaped garden with patio, pergola, water fall, pond and fine views. New plantings. Route: A716 to Drummore; go through village following Mull of Galloway road; the garden is approx. one mile outside village on the right side of a crossroads. Teas. Plant stall.
Admission £1.50 Children under 14 free
SUNDAYS 22 MAY & 26 JUNE 2 - 5pm
Also open at other times by appointment Tel: 01776 840636
40% to Red Cross 60% net to SGS Charities

4. LOGAN HOUSE GARDENS, Port Logan, by Stranraer ♿
(Mr & Mrs Roberts)
Queen Anne house, 1701. Rare exotic tropical plants and shrubs. Fine specie and hybrid rhododendrons. Route: 14 miles south of Stranraer on A716, 2½ miles from Ardwell village.
Admission: £2.00 Children under 16 Free
SUNDAY 1 MAY 9am -6pm
Also open daily: 1 February - 1 april 10am - 4pm   2 April- 31 august 9am - 6pm
Plants, produce etc. for sale.
40% to Port Logan Hall Fund   60% net to SGS Charities

5. LOGAN BOTANIC GARDEN, Port Logan, by Stranraer &

(Regional Garden of the Royal Botanic Garden Edinburgh and one of the National Botanic Gardens of Scotland)

At the south-western tip of Scotland lies, Logan unrivalled as the county's most exotic garden. With a mild climate washed by the Gulf Stream, a remarkable collection of bizarre and beautiful plants, especially from the southern hemisphere, flourish out-of-doors. Enjoy the colourful walled garden with its magnificent tree ferns, palms and borders and the contrasting woodland garden with its unworldly gunnera bog. Explore the Discovery Centre or take an audio tour. Home baking and Botanics Shop. Guide dogs only. Route: 10 miles south of Stranraer on A716, then 2½ miles from Ardwell village.

Admission : £3.50 Concessions £3.00 Children £1.00 Family £8.00

SUNDAY 29 MAY 10am - 6pm

40% to Royal Botanic Garden Edinburgh 60% net to SGS Charities

For further opening details see advert at the back of the handbook

---

6. WOODFALL GARDENS, Glasserton   &

(David and Lesley Roberts)

A 3 acre, 18th Century walled garden undergoing revitalisation. As well as the remains of the original garden buildings there are mixed borders, a woodland area with specimen plants, a parterre, a productive potager, fruit trees and bushes and a specialist boxwood nursery. Weather permitting The Swallow Theatre will perform a short play in the garden commencing at 4pm. Plant stall. Sorry no dogs. 2 miles south of Whithorn junction of A746/747

Admission Adults £2.50 Concessions £2.00 Accompanied children under 14 free

SUNDAY 15 MAY & 3 JULY 2 - 5.30pm

May Opening - 30% to the Swallow Theatre   10% to Glasserton and Isle of Whithorn Church 60% net to SGS Charities

July Opening - 30% Alzheimers (Scotland) 10% to Glasserton and Isle of Whithorn Church 60% net to SGS Charities

---

David and Jane

Branklyn!

All Saints
Glencarse

INCHYRA HOUSE
Glencarse, Perth

GARDEN FAIR

SUNDAY 8th MAY 2005
11.00am - 4.30pm

**An opportunity to view the beautiful grounds and gardens
by kind permission of the owners**
Specialist Plants and Stalls
Soup & Rolls, Teas, Bouncy Castle, Ice Creams

Entrance: Adults £ 3.00

Children: (under 16) 50p

In aid of Hope & Homes for Children & All Saints Episcopal Church, Glencarse

Directions:
From South - M90/A90 to 4 Miles East of Perth, Glencarse slip road - follow signs.
From Dundee - A90 Glencarse/Errol slip road - follow signs
Registered No. SC013463

_So lovely if you come! Binnie Plants
will be there Joey & Jenny —_

137

THE BUCCLEUCH ESTATES
invite you to visit

BOWHILL HOUSE & COUNTRY PARK, Nr Selkirk (Scottish Borders)

18/19th century house in beautiful countryside. Outstanding art collection, fine French furniture and relics of Duke of Monmouth, Sir Walter Scott and Queen Victoria.

Exciting Adventure Woodland Play Area. Audio-visual Visitor Centre. Nature Trails. Picnic Areas. Restored Victorian Kitchen. Licensed Tea Room. Gift Shop.

OPEN 2005

House 1–31 July daily 1–5pm
Country Park Easter, Weekends & Bank Holidays in May & June. Daily with House in July and Daily (except Fridays) in August 11am-5pm
Telephone No: (01750) 22204
Email: bht@buccleuch.com

Off A708 – St. Mary's Loch-Moffat Road 3 miles west of Selkirk. Edinburgh 42 miles, Glasgow 75 miles, Berwick 43 miles, Newcastle 80 mi les, Carlisle 56 miles.

BOUGHTON HOUSE, Nr Kettering (Northamptonshire)

Northamptonshire home of the Dukes of Buccleuch and their Montagu ancestors since 1528. Important art collection, French and English Furniture and Tapestries. "A vision of Louis XIV's Versailles transported to England".

Exciting Adventure Woodland Play Area. Nature Trail. Tea Room. Gift Shop. Plant Centre.

Further details on www.boughton house.org.uk

OPEN 2005

Park 1 May–1 September incl. 1–5 daily, except Fridays. Open Fridays during August with the House.
House and Park 1 August–1 September, 2–4.30 daily. (Park open 1 pm)

Guided Tours in operation on selected dates in August
Tel: (01536) 515731   *Email: llt@boughtonhouse.org.uk*
Off A43, 3 m north of Kettering. Northampton 17m, Cambridge 45 m, Coventry 44 m, Peterborough 32 m, Leicester 26 m, London 50 minutes by train.

DRUMLANRIG CASTLE GARDENS & COUNTRY PARK Nr Thornhill, Dumfriesshire (South-west Scotland)

Castle built 1679-91 on a 15th century Douglas stronghold. Set in parkland ringed by wild hills. French furniture. Paintings by Rembrandt, Holbein and Leonardo. Bonnie Prince Charlie relics.
Gift shop. Licensed Tea Room. Exciting Adventure Woodland Play Area. Picnic Sites. Cycle Hire, Nature Trails. Working Forge. Visitors Centre. Craft Centre.
'Live Wildlife TV 'and woodland walks.

OPEN 2005

Castle 1 May to 21 August Daily 12 - 4pm Guided Tours in operation. Closed Fridays in May and June
Grounds 25 March - 30 September Daily 11am - 5pm
Telephone: (01848) 331555 - Country Park
email: bre@drumlanrigcastle.org.uk
Off A76, 4 miles north of Thornhill. Glasgow 56 miles, Dumfries 18 miles, Edinburgh 56 miles, Carlisle 51 miles.

DALKEITH PARK, Nr Edinburgh (Lothian Region)

Dalkeith Palace not open to public
Nature Trails. Woodland and riverside walks in the extensive grounds of Dalkeith Palace. Tunnel Walk. Adam Bridge. Fascinating Architecture.
Exciting Adventure Woodland Play Area. Picnic Area. Barbecue facilities. Information Centre. Scottish farm animals. Ranger service. Come to our new Cafeteria/Shop in our restored Adam stable.

OPEN 2005

Grounds 25 March–27 October incl. (October - weekends only.) 10 am-6 pm daily
Telephone Nos: 0131-663 5684, 665 3277 or 654 1666
e-mail: dalkeithcountrypark.com
Access from east end of Dalkeith High Street. Off A68, 3 miles from Edinburgh City Boundary.

Parties welcome at all these estates (Special terms and extended opening times for pre-booked parties over 20).
There is no charge for wheelchair users.

SCOTLAND'S GARDENS SCHEME 2005 TOUR

A six day tour to visit gardens in Clydesdale, West Lothian, Ayrshire and Renfrewshire

SUNDAY 26th JUNE - FRIDAY 1st JULY

Telephone 0131 229 1870 for details and brochure

"*Rukba brings a ray of sunshine into my life*"

Rukba, The Royal United Kingdom Beneficent Association, is a charity that champions independence for older people. It provides financial help and friendship to assist people to stay in their homes and we have over 70 volunteer visitors in Scotland who support our beneficiaries. If you would like more information about our work please complete the coupon.

Rukba
in
Scotland

Helping elderly people stay independent

Charity Reg. No.: 210729

TOROSAY CASTLE & Gardens

tea-room • shop • holiday cottages
childrens' adventure playground
free car/coach parking

Relax in the principal rooms of a beautiful Victorian home.
Explore, at your leisure, the interesting gardens
which include water and woodland gardens, an oriental garden
as well as the more formal terraces and impressive Statue Walk.
Enjoy the stunning views over the Sound of Mull to the distant mountains.

TOROSAY CASTLE & GARDENS, Craignure, Isle of Mull, PA65 6AY
Tel: 01680 812421   Fax: 01680 812470
Email: torosay@aol.com   Web site: www.torosay.com

BLAIR CASTLE
5 star attraction set in stunning Highland Perthshire

Within the grounds of Blair Castle is the recently restored walled 'Hercules Garden'
The 10 acre, 18th century formal garden features herbaceous borders, an orchard,
a herb garden and ponds, islands and a Chinese bridge.
Blair Castle's 30 rooms, gift shop and licensed restaurant are open daily from:
19 March - 28 October, 9.30am - 5pm (last entry 4.30pm).

The Castle is situated just off the A9 from Perth to Inverness at Blair Atholl.

Tel: 01796 481207   Fax: 01796 481487

Email: office@blair-castle.co.uk   Web site: www.blair-castle.co.uk

NATIONAL BOTANIC GARDENS OF SCOTLAND

BENMORE BOTANIC GARDEN
Argyll's Magnificent Mountainside Garden

Marvel at giant trees and a world-famous collection of rhododendrons.

- Botanics Shop • James Duncan Cafe
- Courtyard Gallery • Self-guided audio tours

OPEN DAILY, 1 MARCH–31 OCTOBER, 10AM–6PM (CLOSING 5PM IN MARCH & OCTOBER)
7 MILES NORTH OF DUNOON IN ARGYLL, ON THE A815
TEL. 01369 706261 • E-MAIL benmore@rbge.org.uk

LOGAN BOTANIC GARDEN
Scotland's Most Exotic Garden

See tender exotics which can be found in few other gardens in Britain.

- Botanics Shop • Salad Bar • Discovery Centre • Self-guided audio tours

OPEN DAILY, 1 MARCH–31 OCTOBER, 10AM–6PM (CLOSING 5PM IN MARCH & OCTOBER)
14 MILES SOUTH OF STRANRAER IN GALLOWAY, ON THE B7065
TEL. 01776 860231 • E-MAIL logan@rbge.org.uk

DAWYCK BOTANIC GARDEN
Wonderful Woodland Garden

Discover Dawyck's secrets as you explore its wonderful woodland trails.

- The Conservatory for gifts and light refreshments

OPEN DAILY, 1 FEBRUARY–30 NOVEMBER, 10AM–6PM
(CLOSING 4PM IN FEBRUARY & NOVEMBER AND 5PM IN MARCH & OCTOBER)
8 MILES SOUTH-WEST OF PEEBLES IN THE BORDERS, ON THE B712
TEL. 01721 760254 • E-MAIL dawyck@rbge.org.uk

ADMISSION TO THE REGIONAL GARDENS IS: ADULT £3.50, CONCESSION £3, CHILD £1 AND FAMILY £8.

ROYAL BOTANIC GARDEN EDINBURGH
Scotland's Premier Garden

Explore the wonders of the plant kingdom at Inverleith. 28 hectares of beautifully landscaped grounds featuring 10 magnificent Glasshouses.

- Botanics Shop • Terrace Cafe • Guided Tours
- Exhibitions & Events

ENTRY TO THE GARDEN IS FREE WITH AN ADMISSION CHARGE ON THE GLASSHOUSES
OPEN DAILY (EXCEPT 25 DECEMBER & 1 JANUARY) FROM 10AM.
1 MILE NORTH OF THE CITY CENTRE, OFF THE A902 (ENTRANCES OFF INVERLEITH ROW AND ARBORETUM PLACE).
TEL. 0131 552 7171 • E-MAIL info@rbge.org.uk

The Royal Botanic Garden Edinburgh's Mission is to explore and explain the world of plants
www.rbge.org.uk

143

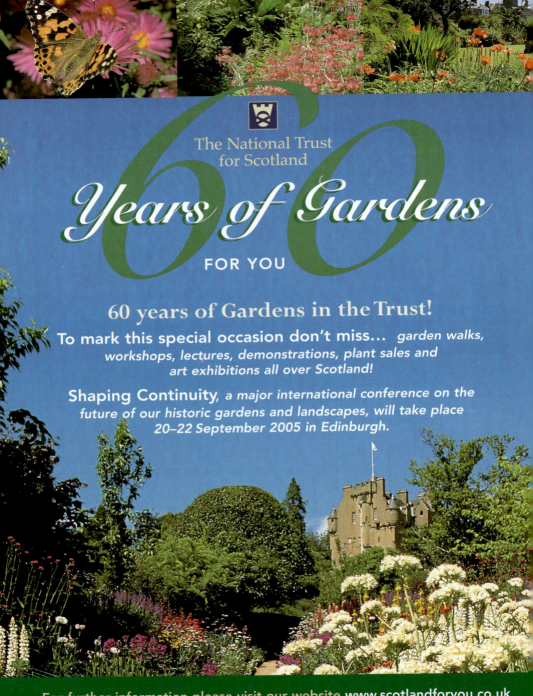

The National Trust
for Scotland

Years of Gardens

FOR YOU

60 years of Gardens in the Trust!

To mark this special occasion don't miss... *garden walks, workshops, lectures, demonstrations, plant sales and art exhibitions all over Scotland!*

Shaping Continuity, *a major international conference on the future of our historic gardens and landscapes, will take place 20–22 September 2005 in Edinburgh.*

For further information please visit our website **www.scotlandforyou.co.uk** Or contact our Customer Services Centre on **0131 243 9300**

Recognised Scottish Charity Number SC 007410

Dumfries & Galloway

Broughton House and Garden

Off A711/A755, at 12 High Street, Kirkcudbright

A fascinating 18th-century house in a delightful harbour town, this was the home and studio from 1901 to 1933 of the artist E A Hornel, one of the 'Glasgow Boys'. His studio overlooks the one-acre Japanese-style garden he designed after visits to the Far East.

OPEN: *GARDEN ONLY: 1 Feb to 31 Mar, daily 11-4. HOUSE AND GARDEN: 1 Apr to 30 Jun and 1 Sep to 31 Oct, daily 12-5; 1 Jul to 31 Aug, daily 10-5.*

Adult	Family	1 Parent	Concession
£8	£20	£16	£5

Threave

Off A75, 1m west of Castle Douglas

Best known for its spectacular daffodils, Threave is also a garden for all seasons, with bright herbaceous beds in summer, and vibrant trees and heather garden in autumn. The Victorian House, now open to visitors, is also home to the Trust's School of Practical Gardening. Visitor Centre with exhibition, shop and licensed restaurant; plant sales, guided walks.

OPEN: *ESTATE All year, daily. WALLED GARDEN AND GLASSHOUSES: all year, daily 9.30-5. VISITOR CENTRE, COUNTRYSIDE CENTRE, EXHIBITION, SHOP AND PLANT CENTRE: 1 Feb to 31 Mar and 1 Nov to 23 Dec, daily 10-4; 1 Apr to 31 Oct, daily 9.30-5.30. RESTAURANT: 1 Feb to 31 Mar and 1 Nov to 23 Dec, daily 10-4; 1 Apr to 31 Oct, daily 10-5. HOUSE: 1 Apr to 31 Oct, Wed, Thu, Fri, Sun 11-3.30.*

Adult	Family	1 Parent	Concession
£10	£25	£20	£7

Scottish Borders

Harmony Garden

In Melrose, opposite the Abbey

Wander through this tranquil garden's herbaceous borders, lawns and fruit and vegetable plots, and enjoy fine views of the Abbey and Eildon Hills.

OPEN: *Good Friday to 30 Sep, Mon-Sat 10-5, Sun 1-5.*

Adult	Family	1 Parent	Concession
£3	£8	£6	£2

Threave

Priorwood Garden and Dried Flower Shop

In Melrose, beside the Abbey

Overlooked by the Abbey ruins, this unique garden produces plants for a superb variety of dried flower arrangements, made and sold here. The orchard contains many historic apple varieties.

OPEN: *SHOP: 6 Jan to 31 Mar, Mon-Sat 12-4; 1 Apr to 24 Dec, Mon-Sat 10-5, Sun 1-5. GARDEN: Good Fri to 24 Dec (same opening times as shop)*

Adult	Family	1 Parent	Concession
£3	£8	£6	£2

Ayrshire and Arran

Brodick Castle, Country Park and Goatfell

Isle of Arran. Ferry: Ardrossan to Brodick (55 mins) connecting bus to Reception Centre (2m). Ferry between Claonaig and Lochranza (north Arran), frequent in summer, limited in winter; tel Caledonian MacBrayne. All-inclusive travel and admission ticket from Strathclyde Passenger Transport Stations (0870) 608 2608.

Built on the site of a Viking fortress and partly dating from the 13th century, this magnificent castle overlooks Brodick Bay and has as a backdrop the majestic Goatfell mountain range. The woodland garden, specialising in rhododendrons, is one of Europe's finest, where plants from the Himalayas, Burma and China flourish. Licensed restaurant, gift shop, plant sales, guided walks.

OPEN: *CASTLE, Good Friday to 31 Oct, daily 11-4.30 (closes 3.30 in Oct). Last admission 30 mins before closing. RECEPTION CENTRE, SHOP AND WALLED GARDEN, Good Friday to 31 Oct, daily 10-4.30; 1 Nov to 21 Dec Fri/Sat/Sun 10-3.30.*

RESTAURANT, *Good Friday to 31 Oct, daily 11-5.*
COUNTRY PARK, *all year, daily.*

Adult	Family	1 Parent	Concession
£10	£25	£20	£7

Culzean Castle and Country Park

12m south of Ayr, on A719, 4m west of Maybole, off A77

One of Scotland's major attractions – a perfect day out for all the family. Robert Adam's romantic 18th-century masterpiece is perched on a cliff high above the Firth of Clyde. The Fountain Garden lies in front of the castle with terraces and herbaceous borders reflecting its Georgian elegance.

The extensive country park offers beaches and rockpools, parklands, gardens, woodland walks and adventure playground. It contains fascinating restored buildings contemporary with the castle. Visitor Centre, shops, plant sales, restaurants and exhibitions. Ranger service events and guided walks.

OPEN: *CASTLE AND WALLED GARDEN, Good Friday to 31 Oct, daily 10.30-5 (last entry 4). VISITOR CENTRE, Good Friday to 31 Oct, daily 9.30-5.30; 1 Nov to 13 Apr, Sat/Sun 11-4. Other visitor facilities, Good Friday to 31 Oct, daily 10.30-5.30. COUNTRY PARK, all year, daily.*

Adult	Family	1 Parent	Concession
£12	£30	£25	£8

Greater Glasgow

Geilston Garden

On the A814 at west end of Cardross, 18m north-west of Glasgow

A delightful garden, laid out over 200 years ago,

and retaining a sense of private space into which the visitor is invited. Attractive features include a walled garden and a burn, winding through the wooded glen.

OPEN: *1 Apr to 31 Oct, daily 9.30-5. House not open.*

Adult	Family	1 Parent	Concession
£5	£14	£10	£4

Greenbank Garden

Flenders Road, off Mearns Road, Clarkston. Off M77 and A726, 6m south of Glasgow city centre

A unique walled garden with plants and designs of particular interest to suburban gardeners. Fountains, woodland walk and special area for disabled visitors. Shop, plant sales, and gardening demonstrations throughout the year.

OPEN: *GARDEN: all year, daily 9.30-sunset. SHOP AND TEAROOM: Good Friday to 31 Oct, daily 11-5; 1 Nov to 31 Mar, Sat/Sun 2-4. HOUSE: Good Friday to 31 Oct, Sun 2-4.*

Adult	Family	1 Parent	Concession
£5	£14	£10	£4

Lothians and Fife

Inveresk Lodge Garden

A6124, near Musselburgh, 6m east of Edinburgh

This sunny hillside garden in the historic village of Inveresk entices visitors with its colourful herbaceous beds, attractive shrubs and old roses selected by Graham Stuart Thomas. Restored Edwardian conservatory with aviary.

OPEN: *All year, daily 10-6 or dusk if earlier.*

Adult	Family	1 Parent	Concession
£3	£8	£6	£2

Malleny Garden

Off the A70, in Balerno, 6m west of Edinburgh city centre

A peaceful walled garden with a collection of old-fashioned roses and fine herbaceous borders. Special features are the 400-year-old clipped yew trees.

OPEN: *All year, daily 10-6 or dusk if earlier.*

Adult	Family	1 Parent	Concession
£3	£8	£6	£2

Malleny Garden

Royal Burgh of Culross

Off A985, 12m west of Forth Road Bridge and 4m east of Kincardine Bridge, Fife

Relive the domestic life of the 16th and 17th centuries amid the old buildings and cobbled streets of this Royal Burgh on the River Forth. A model 17th-century garden has been recreated behind Culross Palace to show the range of plants available and includes vegetables, culinary and medicinal herbs, soft fruits and ornamental shrubs. Shop and tearoom.

OPEN: *PALACE, STUDY, TOWN HOUSE AND SHOP: Good Friday to 30 Sep, daily 12-5. TEAROOM: Good Friday to 30 Sep, daily 11-5. GARDEN: all year, daily 10-6 or sunset if earlier.*

Adult	Family	1 Parent	Concession
£5	£14	£10	£4

Falkland Palace, Garden and Town Hall

A912, 11m north of Kirkcaldy. 10m from M90, junction 8

Set in a medieval village, the Royal Palace of Falkland is a superb example of Renaissance architecture. The stunning gardens were restored to a design by Percy Cane and give a long-lasting display — from spring-flowering cherry trees to the rich autumn colouring of maples. Exhibition and gift shop.

OPEN: *PALACE: 1 Mar to 31 Oct, Mon-Sat 10-6 (last admission 5), Sun 1-5.30 (last admission 4.30). SHOP: 6 Jan to 28 Feb and 1 Nov to 24 Dec, Mon-Sat 11-4, Sun 1-4; 1 Mar to 31 Oct, Mon-Sat 10-6, Sun 1-5.30.*

Adult	Family	1 Parent	Concession
£8	£20	£16	£5

Hill of Tarvit Mansionhouse and Garden

Off A916, 2m south of Cupar

This fine house and garden were rebuilt in 1906 by the renowned Scottish architect Sir Robert Lorimer, for a Dundee industrialist, whose superb collection of furniture is on view. Visitors can wander through the fragrant walled garden, linger on the terraces or enjoy the heady scent of roses in the sunken garden. Shop and tearoom.

OPEN: *HOUSE: Good Friday to 30 Sep, daily 1-5; 1st weekend in Oct, Sat/Sun, 1-5. TEAROOM AND SHOP: same dates but opens at 12 (noon). ESTATE: all year, daily.*

Adult	Family	1 Parent	Concession
£8	£20	£16	£5

Kellie Castle and Garden

On B9171, 3m north of Pittenweem

This superb castle dates from the 14th century and was sympathetically restored by the Lorimer family in the late 19th century. The late Victorian garden has a selection of old-fashioned roses and herbaceous plants, cultivated organically. Shop and tearoom.

OPEN: *CASTLE: Good Friday to Easter Monday and 1 May to 30 Sep, daily 1-5. TEAROOM AND SHOP: same dates but opens at 12 (noon). GARDEN: all year, daily 9.30-5.30. GROUNDS: all year, daily.*

Adult	Family	1 Parent	Concession
£8	£20	£16	£5

Perthshire and Angus

Branklyn Garden

116 Dundee Road, Perth

This attractive garden was first established in 1922. It contains outstanding collections of

Azaleas at Branklyn Garden

rhododendrons, alpines, herbaceous and peat-garden plants and is particularly famed for its *Meconopsis* and its autumn colour.

OPEN: *GARDEN: Good Friday to 30 Oct, daily 10-5.*
SHOP: opening times vary.

Adult	Family	1 Parent	Concession
£5	£14	£10	£4

House of Dun

3 miles west of Montrose on the A935

This beautiful house, overlooking the Montrose Basin, was designed by William Adam in 1730. The restored walled garden displays period herbaceous and rose borders. Shop, restaurant, woodland walks.

OPEN: *HOUSE, SHOP AND RESTAURANT: Good Friday to 30 Jun and 1 to 30 Sep, Wed-Sun (closed Mon and Tue*) 12.30-5.30; 1 Jul to 31 Aug, daily 11.30-5.30. Last admission 45 mins before closing. *NB: Property will be open Bank Holidays from Fri-Mon inclusive.*

Adult	Family	1 Parent	Concession
£8	£20	£16	£5

Aberdeen and Grampian

Castle Fraser and Garden

Off A944, 4m north of Dunecht and 16m west of Aberdeen

One of the grandest Castles of Mar, this magnificent building was completed in 1636 by two master mason families. Walled garden, woodland walks, plant sales, adventure playground, courtyard café and shop.

OPEN: *CASTLE, SHOP AND TEAROOM: Good Friday to 30 Jun, daily (but closed Fri and Mon*)* 12-5; 1 Jul to 31 Aug, daily 11-5; 1 to 30 Sep, daily (but closed Fri and Mon) 12-5. Last admission 45 mins before closing. SHOP also open 1 Nov to 18 Dec, Sat/Sun 12-4. *NB: Property will be open Bank Holidays from Fri-Mon inclusive.*

Adult	Family	1 Parent	Concession
£8	£20	£16	£5

Crathes Castle and Garden

On A93, 3m east of Banchory and 15m west of Aberdeen

Turrets, gargoyles and superb original painted ceilings are features of this enchanting castle, built in the late 16th century. The eight gardens within the walled garden provide a wonderful display all year round. Visitor Centre, restaurant, shop and plant sales, exciting trails and an adventure playground.

OPEN: *CASTLE AND VISITOR CENTRE: Good Friday to 30 Sep, daily 10-5.30; 1 to 31 Oct, daily 10-4.30. Last admission to castle 45 mins before closing. PLANT SALES: same dates, but weekends only in Oct. RESTAURANT and SHOP: 18 Jan to 31 Mar and 1 Nov to 21 Dec, Wed-Sun 10-4; 1 Apr to 30 Sep, daily 10-5.30; 1 to 31 Oct, daily 10-4.30. WALLED GARDEN: all year, daily 9-sunset. GROUNDS: all year, daily.*

Adult	Family	1 Parent	Concession
£10	£25	£20	£7

Drum Castle and Garden

Off A93, 3m west of Peterculter, 8m east of Banchory and 10m west of Aberdeen

The late 13th-century keep, fine adjoining Jacobean mansion house and the additions of Victorian lairds make Drum unique. The Garden of Historic Roses represents different periods of gardening from the 17th to the 20th centuries. Woodland trails, children's playground, shop and tearoom.

OPEN: *CASTLE: Good Friday to 31 May and 1 to 30 Sep, daily 12.30-5.30; 1 Jun to 31 Aug, daily 10-5.30. Last admission 45 mins before closing. GROUNDS: all year, daily.*

Adult	Family	1 Parent	Concession
£8	£20	£16	£5

Fyvie Castle

Off A947, 8m south-east of Turriff and 25m north of Aberdeen

The charm of Fyvie ranges from its 13th-century origins to its opulent Edwardian interiors.

Pitmedden Garden *Arduaine Garden*

Superb collection of arms and armour and paintings, including works by Raeburn and Gainsborough. Stroll around the picturesque lake, or visit the restored 1903 racquet court and bowling alley. Shop and tearoom.

OPEN: *CASTLE: Good Friday to 30 Jun and 1 to 30 Sep, Sat-Wed (closed Thu and Fri*) 12-5; 1 Jul to 31 Aug, daily 11-5. Last admission 4.15. *NB: Property will be open Bank Holidays from Fri-Mon inclusive. GROUNDS: open all year, daily.*

Adult	Family	1 Parent	Concession
£8	£20	£16	£5

Haddo House

Off B999, near Tarves, 19m north of Aberdeen

This elegant mansion house boasts sumptuous Victorian interiors beneath a crisp Georgian exterior. Noted for fine furniture and paintings, Haddo also has a delightul terrace garden, leading to a Country Park with lakes, walks and monuments. Shop, plant sales and restaurant.

OPEN: *HOUSE: Good Friday to Easter Monday 11-4.30; May to Jun, Sat/Sun only 11-4.30; 1 Jul to 31 Aug, daily 11-4.30; Sep, Sat/Sun only 11-4.30. STABLES SHOP AND TEAROOM: Good Friday to 30 Jun, Fri-Mon 11-5; 1 Jul to 31 Aug, daily 11-5; Sep to Xmas Fayre (1st weekend in Nov), Fri-Mon 11-5. GARDEN: all year, daily.*

Adult	Family	1 Parent	Concession
£8	£20	£16	£5

Leith Hall and Garden

On B9002, 1m west of Kennethmont and 34m north-west of Aberdeen

This mansion house was the home for almost 300 years of the Leith family, and the elegantly

furnished rooms reflect their lifestyle. Outside, wander among the glorious herbaceous borders or explore the estate trails. Picnic area and tearoom.

OPEN: *HALL: Good Friday to Easter Monday 12-5; 1 May to 30 Sep, Fri-Tue (closed Wed and Thu) 12-5. Last admission 4.15. GROUNDS and GARDEN: all year, daily.*

Adult	Family	1 Parent	Concession
£8	£20	£16	£5

Pitmedden Garden

On A920, 1m west of Pitmedden village and 14m north of Aberdeen

In the Great Garden, the elaborate original parterre designs of the 17th century have been carefully re-created and are spectacularly filled in summer with some 40,000 annual flowers. Picnic area, shop, tearoom.

OPEN: *GARDEN, MUSEUM of FARMING LIFE, SHOP AND TEAROOM: 1 May to 30 Sep, daily 10-5.30. Last admission at 5. GROUNDS: all year, daily.*

Adult	Family	1 Parent	Concession
£5	£14	£10	£4

Highlands

Arduaine Garden

On A816, 20m south of Oban and 18m north of Lochgilphead

Arduaine boasts spectacular rhododendrons and azaleas in late spring and early summer, but its perennial borders are magnificent throughout the season. Stroll through the woodland to the coastal viewpoint, or relax in the water garden.

Crarae Garden

Inverewe Garden

OPEN: *RECEPTION CENTRE: Good Friday to 30 Sep, daily, 9.30-4.30. GARDEN: all year, daily 9.30-sunset.*

Adult	Family	1 Parent	Concession
£5	£14	£10	£4

Balmacara Estate and Lochalsh Woodland Garden

A87, 3m east of Kyle of Lochalsh

A crofting estate of 6,795 acres with superb views of Skye and Applecross. Lochalsh Woodland Garden enjoys a tranquil setting by the shore of Loch Alsh and has a collection of hardy ferns, fuchsias, hydrangeas, bamboos and rhododendrons.

OPEN: *ESTATE: all year, daily. WOODLAND GARDEN: all year, daily 9-sunset. RECEPTION KIOSK: 1 Apr to 30 Sep, daily 9-5. BALMACARA SQUARE VISITOR CENTRE: 1 Apr to 30 Sep, daily 9-5 (Fri 9-4).*

Pay and display £2

Brodie Castle

Off A96 4¹/₂m west of Forres and 24m east of Inverness

A 16th-century tower house with 17th- and 19th-century additions, Brodie has unusual plaster ceilings, a major art collection, porcelain and fine furniture. In springtime the grounds are carpeted with the daffodils for which the castle is rightly famous.

OPEN: *CASTLE: Good Friday to 30 Apr and 1 Jul to 31 Aug, daily 12-4; 1 May to 30 Jun and 1 to 30 Sep, Sun-Thu 12-4; TEAROOM AND SHOP: same dates as castle, but open 11-4. GROUNDS: all year, daily.*

Adult	Family	1 Parent	Concession
£8	£20	£16	£5

Crarae Garden

A83, 10m south of Inveraray

Set on a hillside down which tumbles the Crarae Burn, this delightful garden is reminiscent of a Himalayan gorge. Tree and shrub collections are rich and diverse. The garden contains one of the best collections of the genus *Rhododendron* in Scotland, unusually rich in cultivars, as well as part of the National Collection of *Nothofagus* and particularly good representations of *Acer, Eucalyptus, Eucryphia* and *Sorbus*. The autumn colours of the leaves and berries are well worth a visit too. Plant sales, shop and tearoom.

OPEN: *VISITOR CENTRE: Good Friday to 30 Sep, daily 10-5. GARDEN: all year, daily 9.30-sunset.*

Adult	Family	1 Parent	Concession
£5	£14	£10	£4

Inverewe Garden

On A832, by Poolewe, 6m north-east of Gairloch

The tallest Australian gum trees in Britain, sweet-scented Chinese rhododendrons, exotic trees from Chile and Blue Nile lilies from South Africa, all grow here in this spectacular lochside setting, favoured by the warm currents of the North Atlantic Drift. Visitor Centre, shop, plant sales, licensed restaurant.

OPEN: *GARDEN: all year, daily 9.30-4; extended hours Good Friday to 31 Oct, daily 9.30-9 or sunset if earlier. VISITOR CENTRE AND SHOP: Good Friday to 30 Sep, daily 9.30-5; 1 to 31 Oct, daily 9.30-4. RESTAURANT: Good Friday to 30 Sep, daily 10-5; 1 to 31 Oct, daily 10-4.*

Adult	Family	1 Parent	Concession
£8	£20	£16	£5

The National Trust
for Scotland

Plants for Sale!

We hope you enjoy your visit to a magical National Trust for Scotland garden.
At some of our gardens we can offer you the perfect souvenir —
a chance to recreate a bit of that garden in your own garden.
We now sell plants from 17 of our garden properties as listed below:

- **Falkland Palace**
- **Glencoe**
- **Greenbank Garden**
- **Inverewe Garden**
- **Pitmedden Garden**
- **Threave Garden**

- **Killiecrankie**
- **Hugh Miller's Cottage**
- **House of Dun**
- **Branklyn Garden**
- **Brodick Castle**
- **Castle Fraser**

- **Crathes Castle**
- **Culzean Castle**
- **Hill of Tarvit**
- **Crarae Garden**
- **Drum Castle**

This varies from a few tables of our home grown plants at some properties,
to a full blown plant centre with a wide selection of shrubs, rhododendrons,
herbaceous plants, alpines and roses at others. Some of the plants
will have been grown in the garden.

We are delighted to be able to offer plants like the famous Primula 'Inverewe'
and Crocosmia 'Culzean Pink'. We also offer a wide selection of bulbs in
season and some of the gardens now produce their own packets of seed.

The next time you visit a National Trust for Scotland property look out
for the exciting range of garden plants on offer.

All the proceeds from the sales contribute to the vital
conservation work of the Trust.

For more information please contact our properties directly.

Index to Gardens

Index to Advertisers

Whichford Pottery

will be selling a large range of their
hand-made flowerpots in the
beautiful Long Gallery at

*Classic Hand-made
English Flowerpots*

Kirknewton House

Kirknewton, West Lothian

(either A71 or A70 on to B7031)

Friday 13th & Saturday 14th May 2005
10am to 5pm

*Whichford Pottery specialise in producing
top quality terracotta flowerpots,
entirely by hand and in every shape and size.
All Whichford pots carry a 10 year frostproof guarantee.*

The extensive gardens at
Kirknewton House will also be open.

*For a mail order catalogue
or more information:*
Whichford Pottery
Whichford
Warwickshire
CV36 5PG
**www.whichfordpottery.com
or telephone 01608 684416**

GARDENS OF SCOTLAND
2006

Order now and your copy will be posted to you on publication in February

Scotland's Gardens Scheme
22 Rutland Square
Edinburgh EH1 2BB

Please send me_____ copy/copies of
"Gardens of Scotland 2006
Price £5.50, to include p&p, as soon as it is available
I enclose a cheque/postal order made payable to
<u>Scotland's Gardens Scheme</u>

Name..

Address..

Postcode....................